PORSCHE

N379-1 SETUBAL

INTRO

Wenn man Portugal in einem Wort beschreiben müsste, dann wäre es wohl: Gegensätze. Modern und traditionell, dynamisch und slow-paced, reichhaltig und einfach, Atlantik und Berge, feucht und trocken, kühl und heiß. Die Liste könnte noch eine ganze Weile fortgeführt werden, aber Worte sind nicht das Lebenselixier von CURVES. Dieses Magazin lebt vom Tun. Vom Losfahren und Entdecken. Vom Selbst-Dortgewesen-Sein. Und deshalb wollten wir uns Portugal einmal ganz intensiv ansehen, sind vom Norden rund um Porto in die Gebirgszüge des Landesinneren gefahren, an der Atlantikküste entlang und hinter Lissabon immer weiter bis in den Süden, an die Algarve. Dabei haben wir ein Portugal entdeckt, das uns vollkommen neu war. Ganz anders als die Bilder und Ideen, mit denen wir uns auf den Weg gemacht haben. Und wir haben uns in die Gegensätze des Landes verliebt, den Moment, in dem man aus den saftig grünen, kühlen Wäldern rund um Sintra an der Atlantikküste landet. In der Sonne, während der Dunst des Ozeans die Luft schillern lässt. Und bereits dieser Moment allein wäre die ganze Reise wert gewesen. Mehr soulful driving geht nicht. Und deshalb: Bem-vindo a Portugal!

—

If you had to describe Portugal in one word, it would have to be: contrasts. Modern and traditional, dynamic and slow-paced, rich and rustic, Atlantic and mountains, damp and dry, cool and hot. The list could go on and on, but words are not the lifeblood of CURVES. This magazine is about doing. About setting off and exploring. About being there in person. And that's why we wanted to take a closer look at Portugal. We drove from the north around Porto into the mountain ranges of the interior, along the Atlantic coast and beyond Lisbon to the south, to the Algarve. We discovered a Portugal that we had never expected. Totally different to the images and ideas we had before we set off. And we fell in love with the contrasts of the country, like the moment we arrived at the Atlantic coast from the lush green, cool forests around Sintra. Standing in the sun, while the haze from the sea makes the air shimmer. And that moment alone would have been worth the entire trip. It's impossible to get driving more soulful than that. And so, bem vindo a Portugal!

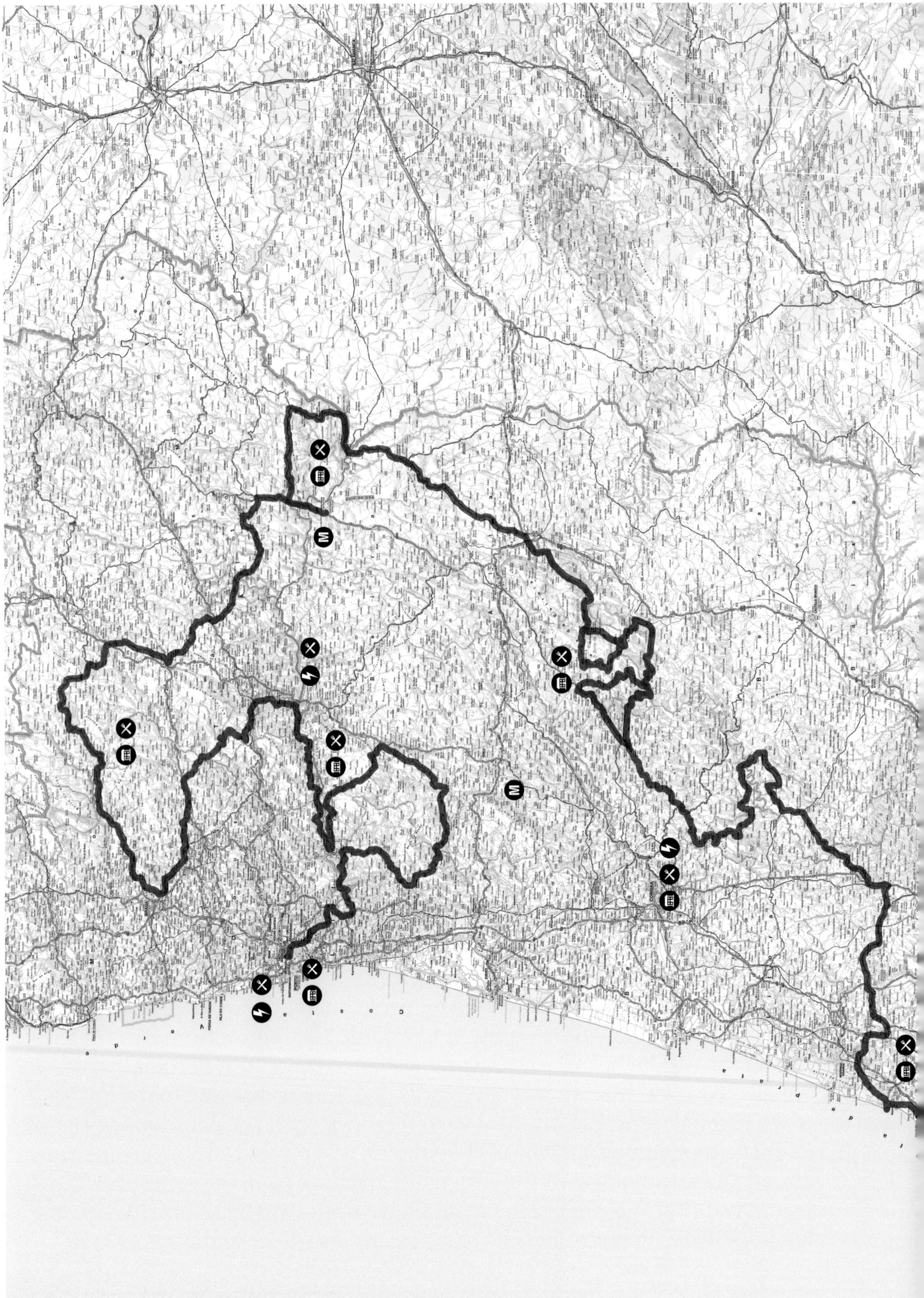
PORTO
MATOSINHOS
MAIA
GONDOMAR
VILA DO CONDE
PÓVOA DE VARZIM

LISBOA
SETÚBAL
BADAJOZ
SEVILLA
HUELVA
Baía de Setúbal
Costa Dourada
Costa Vicentina
Praias do Algarve
Alto Alentejo
Baixo Alentejo
Algarve
Sierra Morena
Parque Nacional de Doñana

MIRADOURO DE SÃO GREGÓRIO

1 ETAPPE STAGE

In Porto, der großen Stadt im Norden Portugals, beginnen wir unsere Tour. Prägender Charakter dieser Etappe wird genau eine Persönlichkeit sein: der Fluss Douro, Lebensader des Nordens, Träger des Portweins. Mit seinen unzähligen Windungen und dem tief eingeschnittenen Tal wird er Begleiter und Hindernis zugleich, an ihm kommen wir nicht vorbei – und wollen es auch nicht. Nördlich und südlich des Flusses sind aber auch menschenleere und majestätische Gebirgslandschaften zu entdecken, die wir in zwei großen Runden erkunden, sie sind voller Fahrfreude und Überraschungen, voller Kurven und von häufig unverfälschtem, rauem Charakter. Am Ende der ersten Etappe haben wir in Vila Nova de Foz Côa beinahe die Grenze nach Spanien erreicht und treffen dort auch wieder auf einen alten Bekannten: den Douro.

We begin our journey in Porto, the large city in northern Portugal. There will be just one distinguishing protagonist on this leg: the Douro River, the lifeline of the north, the bearer of port wine. With its countless twists and turns, its deeply cut valley, it becomes both a companion and a hindrance that we simply can't get past – and we don't want to. To the north and south of the river, however, there are uninhabited and majestic mountain landscapes waiting to be discovered. We do exactly this in two large loops, which are packed with driving pleasure and surprises, full of curves and often with an unspoiled, rough character. At the end of the first leg in Vila Nova de Foz Côa, we've almost reached the border to Spain and there we rendezvous again with an old friend: the Douro.

2 ETAPPE STAGE

Vom östlichen, trockenen Ende der Weinbaugebiete am Douro starten wir unsere zweite Etappe. Folgen der Straße bis ins Grenzgebiet zwischen Spanien und Portugal, und rollen dann in südlicher Richtung davon, immer in Richtung Guarda. Hier haben wir den Fuß der sogenannten Serra da Estrela erreicht, einem Ausläufer des großen Scheidegebirges im Zentrum der iberischen Halbinsel. Während es die Gipfel auf spanischem Territorium bis auf über 2500 Meter Meereshöhe schaffen, erreicht die Serra da Estrela immerhin noch knapp 2000 Meter und ist damit das höchste Gebirge Portugals. Ein beinahe alpiner Charakter und dünne Besiedlung machen unsere Etappe über den Rücken der Serra zur Herausforderung, die wir inklusive der anschließenden Kilometer in Richtung Coimbra gern annehmen. Bei Lousã drehen wir allerdings bei und schlagen einen Bogen um das Fluss-System des Rio Zêzere, ab Sertã streben wir in Richtung Osten. An Tomar vorüber, über Alburitel und Leiria erreichen wir Marinha Grande – die Küste des Atlantik ist nun nur noch 10 Kilometer entfernt.

We begin stage two from the eastern, dry end of the Douro Valley wine region, follow the road to the border of Spain and Portugal, then roll to the south, direction Guarda. Here, we reach the foot of the so-called Serra da Estrela, the foothills of the great dividing range in the centre of the Iberian Peninsula. While the peaks on Spanish territory tower to almost 2,500 meters above sea level, the Serra da Estrela impressively manages just under 2,000 meters and is thus the highest mountain range in Portugal. An almost alpine character and sparse settlements make this stage over the ridge of the Serra somewhat challenging, but that doesn't concern us in the slightest as we head towards Coimbra. At Lousã, however, we heave-to and snake along the river system of the Rio Zêzere. At Sertã, we swing east. Past Tomar, over Alburitel and Leiria, we reach Marinha Grande – the Atlantic coast is now just 10 kilometers away.

3 ETAPPE STAGE

Die Route der dritten Etappe wird vom Meer definiert. Vergessen sind die Berge des Landesinneren – jetzt hat der Atlantik das Sagen. Auf häufig schnurgeraden Straßen rollen wir parallel zur Küstenlinie, es sind die kleinen Fischer- und Bade-Dörfer, die uns immer wieder ans Meer locken, um dort auf den breiten, weißen Stränden das Hochgefühl eines Tags am Meer zu genießen. Aber auch die Klippen und Riffe haben es in sich: In Nazaré sind mit etwas Wetterglück die höchsten Wellen der Erde zu beobachten, die von einer Big-Wave-Surfer-Elite bezwungen werden – oder auch umgekehrt. Und ein paar Kilometer weiter liegt am Cabo da Roca der westlichste Punkt des europäischen Festlands. Mit dem Sintra-Cascais-Naturpark bietet die dritte Etappe ein fantastisches Kontrastprogramm zu den Kilometern am Meer: In schroffen Bergen voller dichtem Grün sammelt sich die Luftfeuchte des Atlantiks und erschafft so eine magische Welt, die mit ihren Schlössern, Klöstern und Mauren-Burgen unbedingt erkundet werden will. In Cascais hat uns dann das Meer wieder – und wir beinahe das Ziel erreicht: Lissabon, die Hauptstadt Portugals wartet auf uns.

The route of the third stage is characterized by the sea. The inland mountains are forgotten, now the Atlantic is in charge. On straight-as-a-die roads we follow the coastline, enjoying the small fishing and seaside villages that constantly beckon to us to come and savor a day at the wide, white beaches. But the cliffs and reefs are also hard to resist. With a bit of luck with the weather, you can watch how the world's best big-wave surfers conquer the highest waves on Earth – or vice versa. Cabo da Roca several kilometers further on is the westernmost point of mainland Europe. Thanks to the Sintra-Cascais Nature Park, leg three offers a fantastic contrast program to the many kilometers of ocean: The humidity of the Atlantic gathers in the rugged hills full of dense foliage, creating a magical world that is irresistible with its castles, monasteries and Moorish fortresses. We meet the ocean again at Cascais – and we've almost reached our destination: Lisbon, Portugal's capital awaits us.

4 ETAPPE STAGE

Lissabon zieht mit seiner Dynamik, Schönheit und Geschichte Besucher aus der ganzen Welt an, die Hauptstadt Portugals mit ihren rund 500.000 Einwohnern ist Startpunkt unserer Etappe. Ohne eine intensive Begegnung mit dieser Stadt ist eine Portugal-Reise kaum denkbar, es lohnt sich, hier auch mehrere Tage einzuplanen. Auf der weiteren Fahrt nach Süden rollen wir über die Halbinsel im Süden und hinein ins Küstengebirge Serra da Arrábida. Dieser Bogen sollte keinesfalls ausgelassen werden, die unter Naturschutz stehende Landschaft ist wunderschön und bietet majestätische Ausblicke auf die Bucht an der Mündung des Rio Sado. Hinter Setúbal macht die Route nach Süden zwei Vorschläge: Entweder umrundet man die Mündung des Sado-Flusses in einem weiten Bogen nach Osten, wer sich jedoch Zeit nimmt, hat mit der Fährfahrt zur vorgelagerten Halbinsel Troia und einer Fortsetzung der Fahrt dicht am Atlantik die landschaftlich eindeutig schönere Wahl getroffen. In Sines statten wir der Geburtsstadt des portugiesischen Seefahrers und Entdeckers Vasco da Gama einen Besuch ab, danach sind wir am Rand des Naturparks Alentejano unterwegs, der bis zur Südwestspitze der iberischen Halbinsel bei Sagres führt.

Lisbon lures visitors from all over the world with its dynamism, beauty and history. The capital of Portugal with its 500,000 or so inhabitants is the starting point for our next leg. A trip to Portugal would be unthinkable without spending a decent amount of time exploring the city. Best to set aside a couple of day for this. On the drive to the south, we roll over the peninsula and into the Serra da Arrábida range. This arc is a must, the protected landscape is stunning and offers majestic views of the bay at the mouth of the Rio Sado. After Setúbal, there are two routes to the south: Either circling the mouth of the Sado River in a wide arc to the east, or, if you have time, catch the ferry to the Troia Peninsula and continue the journey close to the Atlantic. Obviously, the more beautiful option. At Sines, we pay a visit to the birthplace of the Portuguese navigator and explorer Vasco da Gama, then head to the edge of the Alentejano Natural Park, which leads to the south-westerly tip of the Iberian Peninsula near Sagres.

5 ETAPPE STAGE

Der Süden Portugals – das ist Schauplatz der letzten Etappe unserer Reise. Vom São Vicente-Kap bei Sagres bis zur Grenze nach Spanien sind wir unterwegs, fahren diese rund 150 Kilometer Luftlinie natürlich aber nicht auf dem geraden Weg, sondern nehmen uns Zeit für die atemberaubenden Berge der Algarve-Region. Die stehen im Schatten der Strände des Südens, gehören für Reiseende mit CURVES im Herzen aber zu den starken Attraktionen dieser südwestlichsten Ecke Europas. Ein weiter Bogen von Lagos ins Gebirge von Monchique bis wieder hinunter nach Portimão führt uns in entlegene Regionen, auf schmale und verwunschene Straßen, in eine Welt mit gemächlichem Gang. Zurück in der Küstenregion legen wir einen Zwischenstopp ein, der vom exakten Gegenteil geprägt ist: Vollgas. – Die hügelige und vertrackt zu fahrende Rennstrecke von Portimão steht seit Jahren im Kalender der Superbike- und MotoGP-Weltmeisterschaften, 2020 ist sogar die Formel Eins hier zu Gast. Nach dieser schwungvollen Party-Einlage neigt sich unsere Fahrt durch Portugal nun tatsächlich ihrem Ende entgegen, nur noch eine letzte Runde führt uns als Absacker zurück in das stille Land, das wir so sehr ins Herz geschlossen haben – dann landen wir dort, wo alle Geschichten dieser großen Fahrt beginnen und enden: am Meer.

Portugal's south is the scene of the last stage of our trip. We head from Cape St. Vincent near Sagres to the Spanish border – almost 150 kilometers as the crow flies, but not in a straight line, of course. We take our time through the breathtaking mountains of the Algarve region. They lack the fame of the south's beaches, but in keeping with the CURVES spirit, they belong to the major attractions of this south-western corner of Europe. Another wide arc from Lagos into the mountains of Monchique all the way down to Portimão, narrow, magical roads lead us to remote regions, into a world with a leisurely pace. Back at the coast, we make a detour that brings the exact opposite: full throttle. The rollercoaster racetrack of Portimão has hosted Superbike and Moto Grand Prix World Championships for years, and in 2020, even Formula One pays a visit. After this lively party performance, our trip through Portugal is now coming to an end – but just one last lap leads us back to the quiet country that we've come to love. We end up there, where every story of great journeys begins and ends: at the sea.

PARQUE DA BARRAGEM DE ODELOUCA

EDITORIAL

Portugal – das ist das Kalifornien Europas. Nur im Kleinen. Mit magischer und wilder Natur, sonnendurchflutet und vielseitig. Mit spannenden Gegensätzen, einsamen Landregionen und dynamischen Städten. Mit grünem Norden und einem trocken-heißen Süden. Mit dem lebhaften, leidenschaftlichen Kick, den Spanier, Portugiesen, Latein- und Mittelamerikaner gemeinsam haben und der auch „La California" so prägt. Selbst die Surfer, die hier an der grandiosen Atlantikküste unterwegs sind und den Flow suchen, erinnern uns an jene andere Westküste, die viele tausend Kilometer von Portugal entfernt ist. Und natürlich hat jeder Vergleich auch seine Grenzen: Während Kalifornien ein junges und turbulentes Land ist, mitten in den Teenager-Jahren seiner Entwicklung, ist Portugal uralt, weise und melancholisch. Genau dies macht auch den großen Reiz des Landes aus: Man setzt sich gern hin und lauscht den epischen Geschichten von Größe und Verlust, von Euphorie und Versagen, von Schönheit und Tragödie, Liebe und Gewalt, die Portugal zu erzählen hat. Das Land ist ein dramatisches Schwergewicht – und zumindest in dieser Hinsicht völlig anders als das immer noch junge „Popkultur-Phänomen" Kalifornien.

Die großen und kleinen Spannungsbögen einer ungeheuer langen Geschichte sind tief ins kollektive Unterbewusstsein Portugals gewoben. Hinein in die Kultur, ins Lebensgefühl, ins Selbstbewusstsein. Von einer Bevölkerung im schriftlosen Dunst der Vorantike, über Kelten und Römer, über jahrhundertelange maurische Herrschaft und dann die katholischen Königreiche des Mittelalters, über Zeiten des Kolonialismus und der Diktatur bis hin zu einer Moderne, die leidgeprüft und trotzdem überraschend vital ist. Mit Wurzeln, die tief ins Erdreich dringen. Oder etwas weniger sentimental betrachtet: typisch für das alte Europa. Aber dann wäre da eine Besonderheit, der Einfluss eines ewigen Königreichs in unaufhörlicher, prägender Nachbarschaft: das Meer. Wie es ist, immer mit diesem Blick hinaus auf den Ozean zu leben, das können wir Mitteleuropäer nur erahnen. Der Sog des Atlantiks ist unvorstellbar, hier in Portugal hörst du ihn immer. Du lebst im Bewusstsein,

Portugal – Europe's California, only smaller. Magical and wild nature, sun-drenched and multifaceted. With captivating contrasts, remote inland regions and dynamic cities. With the green north and the hot, dry south. With the lively, passionate kick that the Spanish, Portuguese, South and Central Americans have in common and that also characterizes "La California". Even surfers scanning the grandiose Atlantic coastline for waves remind us of that other west coast many thousands of kilometers away from Portugal. But of course every comparison has its limits: While California is a young, turbulent land, still developing and unfolding like a teen, Portugal is old, wise and melancholy. And this is precisely what makes this country so appealing: You like to sit down and listen to the epic stories that Portugal has to tell: tales of greatness and loss, of euphoria and failure, of beauty and tragedy, of love and violence. The country is a dramatic heavyweight – and, at least in this regard, completely different from the still young pop culture phenomenon of California.

The major and minor melodramas of an incredibly long history are woven deep into Portugal's collective consciousness. Into the culture, into the attitude of life, into self-confidence. From a population in the illiterate haze of pre-antiquity, to the Celts and Romans, through centuries of Moorish rule, then the Catholic kingdoms of the Middle Ages, through colonial times and dictatorships to a modern age that is sorely afflicted yet surprisingly vital. With roots penetrating deep into the earth. Or, viewed with a little less sentimentality: Typical for old Europe. But then there is a distinction, the influence of an eternal kingdom in a constant, formative neighborhood: the ocean. We Central Europeans can only imagine was it must feel like to live every day with a view of the ocean. The lure of the Atlantic is unimaginable, here in Portugal its call is constant. You live in the awareness that the world can have no end. That it continues beyond the blue horizon. The great explorers and seafarers of Portugal are as much children of this perception as the times of Portuguese colonialism in Africa, America and

dass die Welt kein Ende haben kann, sondern hinter dem blauen Horizont weitergehen muss. Die großen Entdecker und Seefahrer Portugals sind ebenso Kinder dieser Ahnung wie die Zeiten des portugiesischen Kolonialismus in Afrika, Amerika und Asien. Wie überall auf dieser Welt setzt auch in Portugal eine zunehmend kritische Auseinandersetzung mit diesen Phasen der Geschichte ein, das moderne Portugal stellt sich mittlerweile auch unbequemen Fragen. Für den oberflächlichen Besucher ist das weitgereiste Portugal allerdings eine begeisternde Entdeckung: Auf ganz eigene Weise vermischen sich hier arabische und iberische Elemente mit Einflüssen aus weit entfernten Ländern. Es steckt im Essen, in Kunst und Musik, in Architektur und Kultur, ein Hauch von Exotik und Buntheit schillert unter jeder Oberfläche.

Ohnehin wirkt die portugiesische Seele immer ein wenig fernwehbehaftet. Gerade so, als ob da etwas von einer Seefahrt ans Ende der bekannten Welt nie wieder zurückgekommen wäre. Die Portugiesen sind Kosmopoliten mit selbstbewusst-gelassener Insel-Mentalität – darin ähneln sie auf bemerkenswerte Weise den Isländern, den Nachfahren der Wikinger: Hier und dort verlassen die Jungen das Land, wie Jungfische das Laichgewässer, um dann nach ein paar Jahren auf hoher See zurückzukehren. Wer sich heute in Porto und Lissabon umsieht, wird ähnliche Momente entdecken wie in Reykjavik: Junge Künstler, Köche, Kreative und Geschäftsleute kommen nach einer Karriere in den USA oder in Asien zurück nach Hause, um dort eine bunte, moderne Identität ihres Heimatlandes zu prägen. Fernweh meets Heimweh – das taugt als Kurzbeschreibung für Portugal ebenso wie für Island. (Dass die Portugiesen übrigens eine große Schwäche für nordatlantischen Kabeljau – Island! – haben, muss an dieser Stelle einfach erwähnt werden, die Anekdote ist zu gut, um sie nicht dreist und natürlich ohne jeden Anspruch auf tieferen Sinn einzuwerfen ...) Aber natürlich ist diese Welt zu vielschichtig, um in einfache Zusammenhänge gepresst, oder zu komplex, um mit wenigen Handlungssträngen skizziert zu werden. Und das gilt ganz besonders auch für Portugal: Wer immer mit bestimmten, festgesetzten Erwartungen hierher kam, musste sich ganz schnell überraschen lassen. Portugal kann nicht mit ein paar Kalendermotiven gezeigt oder ein paar Schlagworten beschrieben werden. Wer Sonne und Meer der Algarve im Sinn hat, wird fassungs-

Der Sog des Atlantiks ist unvorstellbar, hier in Portugal hörst du ihn immer. Du lebst im Bewusstsein, dass die Welt kein Ende haben kann.

The lure of the Atlantic is unimaginable, here in Portugal its call is constant. You live in the awareness that the world can have no end.

Asia. Like everywhere else in the world, Portugal is taking an increasingly critical view of these historical phases – and now modern Portugal is also beginning to ask itself uncomfortable questions. For the casual visitor, however, the well-traveled paths of Portugal are inspiring: Arabic and Iberian elements mix here with influences from far-flung lands in a very unique way. It's in the food, in the art and music, in architecture and culture, a touch of exoticism and color shimmers under every surface.

Anyway, the Portuguese soul always seems a little wanderlust-prone. As if something from an ocean voyage to the end of the known world has never returned. The Portuguese are cosmopolitan with a self-confident, relaxed island mentality – in this regard, they are remarkably similar to the Icelanders, the descendants of the Vikings: In both places, the young leave the country, like the juvenile fish in spawning waters, only to return after spending several years on the high seas. If you look around Porto and Lisbon today, you'll discover similar movements to those in Reykjavik: young artists, chefs, creatives and business people return from the USA or Asia to shape a colorful, modern identity in their homeland. Wanderlust meets homesickness – that pretty much sums up both Portugal and Iceland. (The fact that the Portuguese have a soft spot for North Atlantic cod – from Iceland! – simply has to be mentioned at this point. This anecdote is just too good not to be cheekily thrown in here without any claim to having a deeper meaning...)

But of course this world is too multifaceted to be squeezed into simple contexts, or too complex to be summarized in just a few storylines. And this is especially true for Portugal: Every-

los auf die schneebedeckten Gebirgszüge des Nordens schauen. Wer die wehmütige Tiefe des Fado und alter Traditionen verehrt, wird vom digitalen Drive und der unbekümmerten Moderne des Landes überrascht sein. Wer von den Trend-Aposteln des internationalen Travel-Hipstertums nach Lissabon – oder mittlerweile angesagt: Porto – geschickt wird, dürfte die stoische und welt-desinteressierte Konservativität mancher Gegenden Portugals als große Herausforderung empfinden. Und trotzdem gehört all das zu Portugal. Zu seiner Schönheit, seiner Tiefe, seiner Spannung. Es empfiehlt sich daher beim Reisen ein möglichst ergebnisoffener Zugang, der Überraschungseffekt wird trotzdem noch immer maximal sein. Einfach weil Portugal das im Blut hat. Der Wechsel zwischen den Landschaften ist immer wieder atemberaubend, die Schönheit im Detail wirklich berührend und ein konzentriertes Verharren in den Momenten lohnt sich ebenso wie eine hypnotische Fahrt mit weit offenen Sinnen. Am Ende der Reise werden sich dann selbst äußerst meinungsstarke Menschen schwer damit tun, Favoriten zu küren: Die großen und kleinen Städte Portugals haben allesamt eine wundersame Anziehungskraft, die Landschaften der Berge und Hügel sind mindestens ebenso anziehend und geheimnisvoll wie die Küsten. Nur eines werden alle Portugal-Reisenden gleich empfinden: Wer dieses Land einmal gesehen und erlebt hat, wird wiederkommen. Portugal streichst du auf deiner Bucket-List niemals ab. Check, erledigt? – Von wegen.

Selbst die notorisch verwöhnte CURVES-Mannschaft ist nach vielen Tagen und Kilometern quer durch Portugal am Ende wieder am Anfang der Reise: Wir wollen zurück unter den Himmel von Sintra, zurück in die Gassen von Porto, zurück in die Gischt des Atlantiks, zurück in die roten Höhlenbuchten der Algarve, zurück an den Douro, zurück an die Hügel Lissabons, zurück mit der Nase in einen warmen Fahrtwind voller Verheißungen. – Vielleicht ist es ja so, dass das Fernweh-/Heimweh-Syndrom Portugals höchst ansteckend ist. Dass man hier seine Seefahrer-Gene entdeckt, weit weg fährt und am Ende doch immer wieder den Bug mit Kurs Portugal ausrichtet. Zurück nach Hause. An den Mittelpunkt der Welt.

one who came here with certain, fixed expectations very quickly got a big surprise. Portugal cannot be shown with a few calendar photos or described with a few catchphrases. Those thinking just of sun and sea at the Algarve will be astonished to discover snow-capped mountain ranges in the north. Those who love the wistful depths of Fado and old traditions will be surprised by the digital drive and the carefree modernity of the country. And those who are sent to Lisbon – or the now popular Porto - by the trend apostles of the international travel hip, are likely to find the stoic and world-weary conservatism of some areas a big challenge. And yet, all of this belongs to Portugal – to its beauty, its depth, its suspense.

So, the best approach when traveling here is to take an open-minded attitude – the surprise effect will still be huge. Simply because Portugal has it in its blood. The change between landscapes is breathtaking, the beauty in the detail completely poignant and staying put and focusing on the moment is as worthwhile as the hypnotic journey with all senses wide open. By the end of the trip, even the most opinionated traveler will find it difficult to choose favorites: the large and small cities of Portugal all have a magical allure, the landscapes of the mountains and hills are as attractive and mysterious as the coastlines. One thing that all visitors to Portugal will have in common: once they have seen and experienced this country, they will want to return. Portugal can never be ticked off a bucket list. Check, done? No way.

Even the notoriously spoiled CURVES team is finally back to the starting point of the journey after many days and kilometers through Portugal... and already we yearn to return to the skies of Sintra, to the seaspray of the Atlantic, to the red-caved bays of the Algarve, to the Douro, back to the hills of Lisbon, with our noses in the warm wind filled with promise. Perhaps the wanderlust/homesickness syndrome of Portugal is highly contagious. To discover your seafaring genes here, to travel far from the shores and ultimately to keep turning the bow back to Portugal. Back home. To the center of the world.

SERRA DA ESTRELA NATURAL PARK

PARQUE DA BARRAGEM
DE ODELOUCA

SERRA DA ESTRELA
NATURAL PARK

NEAR COMPORTA

PARQUE DA BARRAGEM DE ODELOUCA

MIRADOURO DE SÃO GREGÓRIO

BARRAGEM DO ALTO RABAGÃO

LAGOS

DOURO

AT SINTRA

AUTÓDROMO INTERNACIONAL DO ALGARVE

MIRADOURO DAS AZENHAS DO MAR

PRAIA DE
MONTE CLÉRIGO

PORTO VILA NOVA DE FOZ CÔA

700 KM • 11 STUNDEN // 435 MILES • 11 HOURS

Markerschütterndes Quietschen. Metallisches Mahlen. Ein tiefes Rumpeln, das durch den Boden unter dir, in die Beine und dann bis in alle Knochen dringt. Dann steht er vor dir, der Straßenbahnwagen der Linha 1, der „Electrico". Nichts wie hinein. An einer blankpolierten Holzreling oder den Griffschlaufen festhalten, die an mürben Lederschlaufen von der Kabinendecke hängen, und dann die Fahrt aufsaugen.

—

Bloodcurdling screeching. Metallic grinding. A deep rumble that vibrates from the ground into your legs and finally rattles every bone in your body. There it stands before you; the Linha 1 tram, the "Electrico". We get in, grasp the highly polished wooden railing or the hooped handholds that hang on timeworn leather straps from the cabin ceiling, and soak up the ride.

HOTELS

PORTO A.S. 1829 HOTEL
LARGO SÃO DOMINGOS 45 55,
4050-097 PORTO

CASA DO CATIVO
UNIÃO DE FREGUESIAS
DO CENTRO, R. DO CATIVO 32,
4000-160 PORTO
WWW.CASADOCATIVO.COM

ARMAZÉM LUXURY HOUSING
LARGO SÃO DOMINGOS,
Nº 74, 4050-545 PORTO
WWW. ARMAZEMLUXURYHOUSING.COM

RESTAURANT

DOP RESTAURANTE
PALÁCIO DAS ARTES
LARGO DE S. DOMINGOS, 18
4050-545 PORTO
WWW.DOPRESTAURANTE.PT

CASA DE CHÁ DA BOA NOVA
AVENIDA DA LIBERDADE Nº 1681
4450-718 LEÇA DA PALMEIRA
WWW.CASADECHADABOANOVA.PT

ALMEJA
RUA FERNANDES TOMÁS 819
4000-219 PORTO
WWW.ALMEJAPORTO.COM

Wie ein pummeliges, tumbes Tier aus Stahl, Holz und Messing schiebt sich der Wagen am Ufer des Douro entlang. Unter den Steilhängen und Klippen des Flussufers, vorbei an Lagerhallen und Kasernengebäuden und dann unter der Autobahnbrücke Ponte Arrábida hindurch. Ein paar Meter noch, dann drängt sich Porto heran, schmale Gassen zweigen ins Getümmel der Stadt hinein ab. In den Fenstern des Wagens zieht buntes, turbulentes Leben vorüber. Kopfsteinpflaster wölbt sich über Gehsteige, Cafés, Bäckereien und Kioske atmen ein wahres Gewirr von Menschen ein und aus. Man könnte Porto ja auch zu Fuß erkunden oder sich wie die pragmatischen Einwohner auf die viel moderneren Busse verlegen, aber die alten Tram-Linien sind für Besucher einfach viel schöner. Als Tourist hast du Zeit, willst du etwas sehen, also nimmst du diese herrlich archaischen und gefühlsechten Ungetüme gern mit. Sie passen zu Porto ausgezeichnet – und sie gehören beinahe zwingend an den Beginn dieser Reise durch Portugal. Stellst du glückselig fest, während du schlingernd im Abteil stehst und dich mit Haut und Haaren dieser stampfenden Fortbewegung überlässt.

Hinter uns verschwindet der Atlantik mit seiner sandigen Küste, mit den Surfern auf weiß gischtenden Wellen und jenem glasigen Dunst, der so zu dieser wilden Küste im äußersten Westen des europäischen Kontinents gehört. Und jetzt hat die Reise begonnen. Im schmalen Tal des Douro, das sich hier als Felsrinne in der Stadt Porto dem Ozean entgegenschiebt. Am Palácio da Bolsa versickert die Straßenbahntrasse einfach, du springst aus

Like a stout, dim-witted animal of steel, wood and brass, the tram car trundles along the banks of the Douro. Below the steep slopes and cliffs of the riverbank, past warehouses and barracks, then under the Ponte Arrábida motorway bridge. In a few more meters, Porto presses in, with narrow lanes branching off into the bustle of the city. A colorful, chaotic life passes by the windows of the tram. Cobblestones arch over sidewalks, cafés, bakeries and kiosks inhale and exhale a veritable tangle of people. One could explore Porto on foot or, like the pragmatic locals, take the modern bus, but the old tram lines are simply much nicer for visitors. As a tourist, you have time, you want to explore, so you're more than happy to take a ride on this archaic, sentimental beast. The trams fit Porto perfectly – and they are almost a must-do at the beginning of a trip through Portugal. You blissfully realize this as you stand lurching in the compartment and surrender completely to the pitch and roll of the ride.

Behind us, the Atlantic and its sandy beaches disappear, with the surfers on white, frothing waves and the glazy haze that epitomizes this wild coast on the outer western edge of the European continent. The journey has now begun. In the narrow Douro Valley, cut into the rocks as a home for Porto and now opening up to the ocean. At the Palácio da Bolsa, the tram route simply seeps away. You leap from the car and stroll north. Into the city. Draw a deep breath: hello Porto. Lines of streets with house facades, with only a narrow strip of blue sky above, follow the rise and fall of the city's hills. Shiny Azulejos are everywhere, the small, ceramic tiles glazed with blue patterns forming large mosaic murals. Churches and offices, colorful and lively. And now we're hungry. Here, that

VESTIR BEM
E BARATO
SÓ AQUI
TOURIST SERVICE
TICKET OFFICE
in travel
TICKET OFFICE
TOURIST SERVICE

dem Wagen, schlenderst dann nach Norden. Hinein in die Stadt. Tief durchatmen: Hallo Porto. Straßenzeilen mit Hausfassaden, die über uns nur einen schmalen Streifen Himmel freilassen, streben die Hügel der Stadt hinauf und hinunter. Die glänzenden Azulejos sind überall, kleine, mit blauen Mustern glasierte Keramik-Kacheln, die sich zu großen Wandbildern formieren. Kirchen und Kontore, bunt und lebendig. Und jetzt haben wir Hunger. Was hier so viel heißt wie: ein Rendezvous mit der „kleinen Französin". Die ist weder französisch noch klein, noch irgendwie weiblich, aber wenn du erst einmal Witterung aufgenommen hast und auf sie zusteuerst, ist das alles Nebensache. Zumal die dralle „Francesinha" volle Hingabe fordert: Mächtige Toastscheiben werden zusammen mit einem Stapel auf Passung geschnittener portugiesischer Wurst angebraten, nebenan auf der heißen Platte grillen stabile Schinkenscheiben und saftige Hackfladen. Zwei, drei energische Schubse mit dem Grillwender, und schon segeln die zischenden Einzelteile auf ihre ungebräunte Oberseite, wenige Sekunden später dürfen sie zusammen mit sanft schmelzenden Käsescheiben einen appetitlichen Stapel bilden. Eine weitere Toastscheibe rundet den Cholesterin-Turm ab – bis hierhin dürfte das Ganze noch als obszöne Variante eines Sandwichs für Gemüse-Verächter gelten. Aber nicht lange. Denn jetzt beginnt die Metamorphose zur Francesinha: Ein Spiegelei klettert auf die Spitze, muss diese Position aber an eine weitere Schicht Käse abgegeben, der Fäden ziehend links und rechts bis auf den Teller hängt. Einen tiefen Teller. Denn kurz bevor sich dieses Ungetüm aus Fett und Geschmack auf seinen dampfenden Weg zum Tisch des lüstern schielenden Essers macht, wird es mit einer scharfen Soße übergossen, die später das Innere tränken darf. Die genauen Zutaten der Soße sind Geheimsache des jeweiligen Restaurants, es könnte sich allerdings um

means we'll enjoy a rendezvous with the "little Frenchie". She is neither French nor little, and certainly not feminine, but once you've picked up the scent and made a beeline for it, everything else becomes irrelevant. Particularly because the buxom Francesinha demands your full commitment: Thick slices of bread are grilled alongside a stack of Portuguese sausage cut to size, next to them fry a sturdy slice of ham and juicy meat patties.

Two, three hearty flips with the spatula, and the hissing parts sail onto their unbrowned side, a few seconds later they are mouth-wateringly piled together with gently melting cheese slices. Another slice of toasted bread tops the cholesterol tower – at this point, the whole shebang should be considered an obscene version of a sandwich for vegetable haters. But not for long. Now comes Francesinha's crowning glory: A fried egg is added, but its top position is usurped by another slice of cheese, the molten strings oozing down the sides of the tower to the plate. A deep plate, because shortly before this monster of fat and taste wafts its way to the table of the salivating, ogle-eyed diner, a hot sauce is poured over it, which eventually soaks right through. Restaurants keep the exact ingredients of the sauce a secret – however, it is thought to be a mixture of tomato, mustard and beer. At this point, silence falls over the table, except for a juggle and gobble, a slavering and smacking of lips, disappearing arm in arm with Francesinha into a cloud of happiness.

It will take quite a bit to walk lunch off, so why not tackle the 225 steps to the 76-meter-high Torre dos Clérigos or a crossing of the Ponte Dom Luís I, which spans the Douro Valley like a felled Eiffel Tower. Here it is, the enduring image of Porto: the grayish-green river, besieged and watched by the city's houses. And this sight keeps us

HOTELS

CASA ALTAMIRA
DA LAVRA - ESPADANEDO
4690-119 CINFÃES
WWW.CASAALTAMIRA.PT

QUINTA DE SÃO BERNARDO
CAMINHO DO RIO 33, VILA JUSÃ
5040-428 MESÃO FRIO
WWW.QUINTADESAOBERNARDO.COM

RESTAURANT

DOC RESTAURANTE
ESTRADA NACIONAL 222 – FOLGOSA
5110-204 ARMAMAR
WWW.DOCRESTAURANTE.PT

N304 PARDELHAS

N304 PARDELHAS

N304
156

eine Mischung aus Tomate, Senf und Bier handeln. Ab dann herrscht an den Tischen Schweigen, man kämpft und schlingt, knuspert und schmatzt, verschwindet Arm in Arm mit der Francesinha in einer Wolke aus Glück.

Der Verdauungsspaziergang darf lang sein, gern die 225 Stufen zum 76 Meter hohen Torre dos Clérigos beinhalten oder eine Überquerung der Ponte Dom Luís I. anschließen, die wie ein gefällter Eiffelturm das Douro-Tal überspannt. Das ist sie, die Erinnerung an Porto: Der graugrüne Fluss, belagert und belauert von den Häusern der Stadt. Und dieser Anblick bleibt für die nächsten Kilometer unser Begleiter: Das Tal des Douro, tief eingeschnitten und sich Kehre um Kehre durchs Land windend. Auch ohne die Häuser Portos. Hinter der Ponte do Freixo tritt die Stadt zurück, jetzt ist der Fluss frei und er kommt aus dem einsamen Inneren des Landes, in das wir nun fahren wollen. Bis zum Staudamm bei Lever bleiben wir am Nordufer, dann geht es ans Südufer und dort auf das umgebende Plateau. Nur wenige Kilometer, eine Windung später schwingt die Straße zurück zum Fluss, und dann verlassen wir den Douro bei Olveira do Arda erneut, dieses Mal für viele Stunden, für einen großen Loop über die Berge im Inneren des Landes: Über Pejão und Paraduça geht es geradewegs in Richtung Südosten, die Landschaft wird nun einsam und wild. Herbe Hügel stellen sich der Straße in den Weg und zwingen sie zu einem Kurs, der entlang der Täler führt, in schwingenden Halbhöhen. Als schmales und brüchiges Asphaltband schnüffelt die N224 dahin, der Talboden ist ihr zu wild, die Hügelkuppen zu hoch und deshalb schiebt sie einen selbstvergessenen Tanz mit sich selbst. Immer weiter. Überwuchert von Gestrüpp und überragt von Eukalyptusbäumen, deren Rinde in groben

company for the next few kilometers: the Douro Valley, deeply gouged and winding bend after bend through the countryside. Soon without Porto's houses. After the Ponte do Freixo, the city recedes, now the river flows freely, coming from the lonely interior of the country – where we now want to drive. We stay on the northern bank until the dam near Lever, before switching to the south side and its surrounding plateau. Just a handful of kilometers and a river bend later, the road returns to the Douro.

We again leave the river at Olveira do Arda, this time for many hours, and carve a wide loop over the mountain into the country's interior: over Pejão and Paraduça, we head directly to the southeast, where the landscape turns isolated and wild. Bleak hills block the way of the road, forcing it to take a course along the valleys at sweeping half-heights. The N224, a narrow, brittle strip of asphalt, sniffs and snuffles its way along, the valley floor seems too wild for it, the hilltops too high, and thus, it shuffles as if in an absent-minded dance with itself. On and on. Overgrown by scrub and overhung by eucalypts, the bark of which hangs in ragged strips.

We briefly dive back into civilization near Burgo, only to return to the mountains on the other side of the valley – and we want to. An expansive landscape high under the sky stretches into the distance, the road timidly meandering. It feels as if the road could dissolve into a last breath of gravel at any moment. As if this narrow byway has no official right to exist, as if it were simply tolerated. Low clouds drift by, blue hills evaporate in the distance. Small stands of conifers with black bark and burnt crowns comfort themselves from the last bushfire, even the lone birches have strayed up here, as if they were pale tourists from Scandi-

HOTELS

FARM BARBEDO
RUA DE BARBÊDO
N.º435, 4850-045 CANIÇADA
WWW.QUINTA-BARBEDO.COM

BARRAGEM DO ALTO RABAGÃO

BARRAGEM DO ALTO RABAGÃO

Streifen herabhängt. Kurz tauchen wir bei Burgo zurück in die Zivilisation, müssen dann aber auf der anderen Talseite erneut in die Berge – und wollen es auch: Eine offene Landschaft hoch oben unter dem Himmel treibt hier in die Ferne, die Straße schnürt schüchtern dahin. Jeden Moment könnte sie sich in einem letzten Schotterhauch auflösen, so fühlt sich das an. Als hätte diese schmale Fahrbahn keine offizielle Daseinsberechtigung, als wäre sie nur geduldet. Tief hängende Wolken treiben dahin, in der Ferne verdunsten blaue Hügel. Kleine Gruppen von Nadelbäumen trösten sich mit schwarzen Rinden und kahlen Kronen über das letzte Buschfeuer hinweg, selbst einzelne Birken haben sich hier hinauf verirrt, als wären es blasse Touristen aus Skandinavien. Immer weiter geht das so, bis wir bei Cepelos erneut auf Siedlungen treffen – und erneut beidrehen. In die Berge. Endlose Kurven, ein kurzer Sprung über das Tal des Rio Teixeira, südlich von Valadares über den Rio Vouga und dann die Etappe bis São Pedro del Sul. Zurück nach Norden, zurück zum Douro.

So herrlich diese meditative Runde über das Gebirge im Osten der Stadt Porto war, so sehr suchen wir nun eine zweite Geschichte, für die wir zurück ins Tal des Douro müssen. Am Zufluss des Tâmega fahren wir zurück ans Nordufer und folgen dem Flusstal in Richtung Ribadouro. Hoch oben über dem grünen Strom segelt die Straße in den Terrassen der Uferhänge dahin, huscht um blinde Bögen, schlängelt sich durch eine fette, feuchte Vegetation und mogelt sich wild kurvend durch das scheinbare Chaos der versprengten Garten-Grundstücke. Das Land ist nun üppig und grün. Feigen wachsen hier, Weinberge schmiegen sich in die Kehren des Douro, und das ist erst der Anfang. Weiter im Landesinneren, wo der kühle und feuchte Einfluss des Atlantiks endgültig seine Kraft verliert, hinter der Brücke bei Ermida, warten die Weinberge,

navia. And it continues like this until we finally reach settlements again near Cepelos – only to turn back again. Into the mountain. Endless curves, a short leap over the valley of Rio Teixeira, south of Valadares over the Rio Vouga and then the leg to São Pedro del Sul. Back north, back to the Douro. As delightful as this meditative loop over the mountains to the east of Porto city was, we're now looking for a second story, and for this, we must return to the Douro Valley. Where the Tâmega joins the Douro, we head back to the northern bank and follow the river valley towards Ribadouro. High above the green river, the road sails along slope's terraces, scurrying around blind bends, snaking through rich, damp vegetation and wildly looping around the apparent chaos of scattered garden plots. The land turns lush and green. Figs grow here, vineyards nestle into the bends of the Douro – and that's just the beginning. Further inland, where the cool, humid influence of the Atlantic finally loses its strength, after the bridge at Ermida, the vineyards await from where sweet and heavy nectar goes all over the world.

The Douro Valley and the adjoining river valleys have become the womb of port wine. On steep slopes reaching from 80 to 800 meters in height, the sunny, hot climate of the Iberian Peninsula turns even the north-facing slopes into productive terrain. And what terrain: the expansive snaking of the Douro Valley, with vineyards lining the slopes for as far as the eye can see, row upon row of vines, stretching almost endlessly. Wine has been grown here since time immemorial; the man-made cultural landscape has long since become its true character.

We cover many kilometers in amazement, almost in reverence, and allow this image to sink in all the way to Paso da Régua. Here, the time has come. Here, we take a last,

HOTELS

LONGROIVA HOTEL RURAL
LUGAR DO ROSSIO
6430-071 PORTUGAL
WWW.HOTELDELONGROIVA.COM

MUSEUM

MUSEU E PARQUE ARQUEOLÓGICO DO VALE DO CÔA (MUSEU DO CÔA)
RUA DO MUSEU
5150-620 VILA NOVA DE FOZ CÔA
WWW.ARTE-COA.PT

MIRADOURO DE SÃO GREGÓRIO

MUSEU E PARQUE ARQUEOLÓGICO DO VALE DO CÔA

Seit der Antike wird hier Wein angebaut, die vom Menschen geprägte Kulturlandschaft ist längst zum eigentlichen Charakter geworden. Viele Kilometer fahren wir staunend und beinahe andächtig dahin und lassen dieses Bild auf uns wirken, bis Paso da Régua.

aus denen ein süßer und schwerer Saft in die ganze Welt geht. Das Tal des Douro und die angrenzenden Flusstäler werden zum Schoß des Portweins. Auf Steilhängen, die von 80 Metern bis auf 800 Meter Höhe reichen, wachsen Reben – das sonnige und heiße Klima der iberischen Halbinsel lässt dabei selbst die nach Norden ausgerichteten Hänge zu ertragreichen Lagen werden. Was für ein Anblick: die raumgreifende Schlange des Douro-Tals, an den Hängen Weinberge so weit das Auge reicht, Reben in Reih und Glied, beinahe endlos. Seit der Antike wird hier Wein angebaut, die vom Menschen geprägte Kulturlandschaft ist längst zum eigentlichen Charakter geworden. Viele Kilometer fahren wir staunend und beinahe andächtig dahin und lassen dieses Bild auf uns wirken, bis Paso da Régua.

Hier ist es soweit, hier beginnt für uns ein letzter, weiter Bogen nach Norden, der die erste Etappe abschließen soll. Wir folgen dem Corgo-Tal, erneut begleitet von Weinbergen, dann stechen wir westlich von Vila Real weiter nach Norden. Vorbei am Alvão-Naturpark, unzählige Kurven aneinanderreihend, und dann hinüber nach Braga. Von hier aus werden wir dem Lauf des Cãvado folgen, wechseln dann ins Tal des Rabagão mit seinen großen Stauseen. Fliegen schließlich zurück nach Südosten, viele, viele Kilometer weit, bis wir nahe der Grenze nach Spanien Vila Nova de Foz Côa erreicht haben. Staubbedeckt, sonnengetränkt, mit Hitze aufgeladen. Was für ein Ritt.

Wine has been grown here since time immemorial; the man-made cultural landscape has long since become its true character. We cover many kilometers in amazement, almost in reverence, and allow this image to sink in all the way to Paso da Régua.

long loop to the north, which will conclude the first leg. We follow the Corgo Valley, again accompanied by vineyards, then to the west of Vila Real we continue north. Past the Alvão Natural Park, countless curves one after the other and then over to Braga.

From here, we follow the course of the Cãvado, then switch to the Rabagão Valley with its mighty reservoirs. Finally, we fly many, many kilometers back to the southeast until we reach Vila Nova de Foz Côa close to the Spanish border. Dust-covered, sun-soaked and fired-up with heat. What a journey.

PORTO VILA NOVA DE FOZ CÔA

In Porto, der großen Stadt im Norden Portugals, beginnen wir unsere Tour. Prägender Charakter dieser Etappe wird genau eine Persönlichkeit sein: der Fluss Douro, Lebensader des Nordens, Träger des Portweins. Mit seinen unzähligen Windungen und dem tief eingeschnittenen Tal wird er Begleiter und Hindernis zugleich, an ihm kommen wir nicht vorbei - und wollen es auch nicht. Nördlich und südlich des Flusses sind aber auch menschenleere und majestätische Gebirgslandschaften zu entdecken, die wir in zwei großen Runden erkunden, sie sind voller Fahrfreude und Überraschungen, voller Kurven und von häufig unverfälschtem, rauem Charakter. Am Ende der ersten Etappe haben wir in Vila Nova de Foz Côa beinahe die Grenze nach Spanien erreicht und treffen dort auch wieder auf einen alten Bekannten: den Douro.

—

We begin our journey in Porto, the large city in northern Portugal. There will be just one distinguishing protagonist on this leg: the Douro River, the lifeline of the north, the bearer of port wine. With its countless twists and turns, its deeply cut valley, it becomes both a companion and a hindrance that we simply can't get past - and we don't want to. To the north and south of the river, however, there are uninhabited and majestic mountain landscapes waiting to be discovered. We do exactly this in two large loops, which are packed with driving pleasure and surprises, full of curves and often with an unspoiled, rough character. At the end of the first leg in Vila Nova de Foz Côa, we've almost reached the border to Spain and there we rendezvous again with an old friend: the Douro.

700 KM • 11 STUNDEN // 435 MILES • 11 HOURS

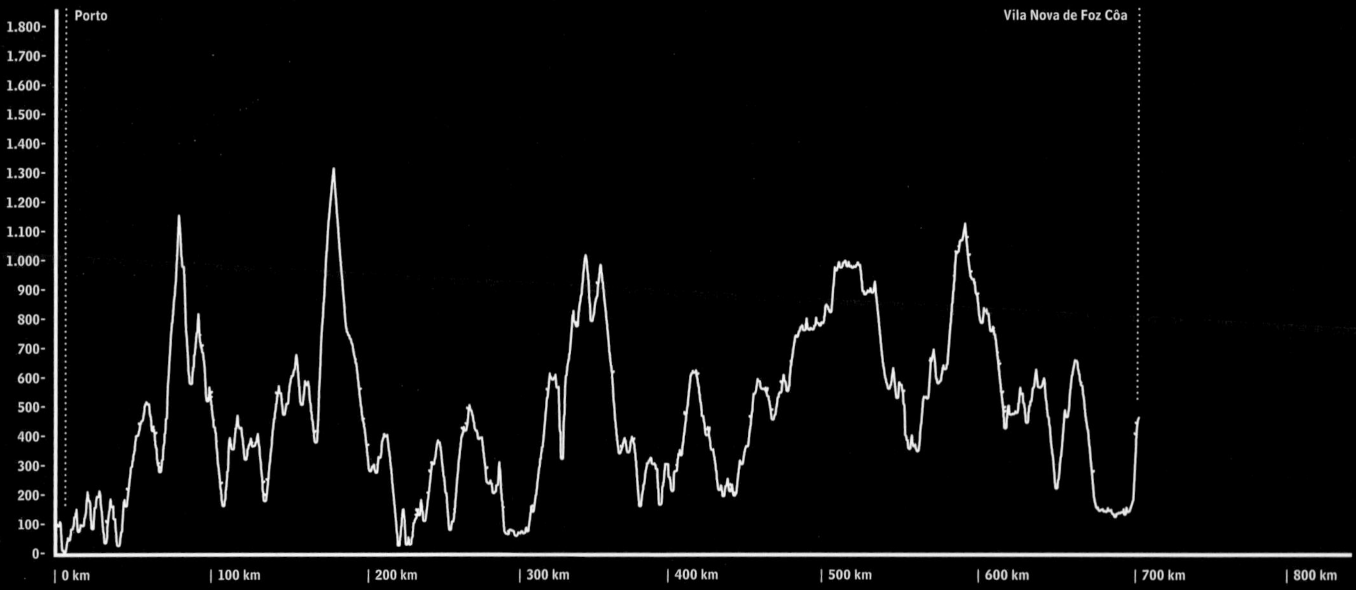

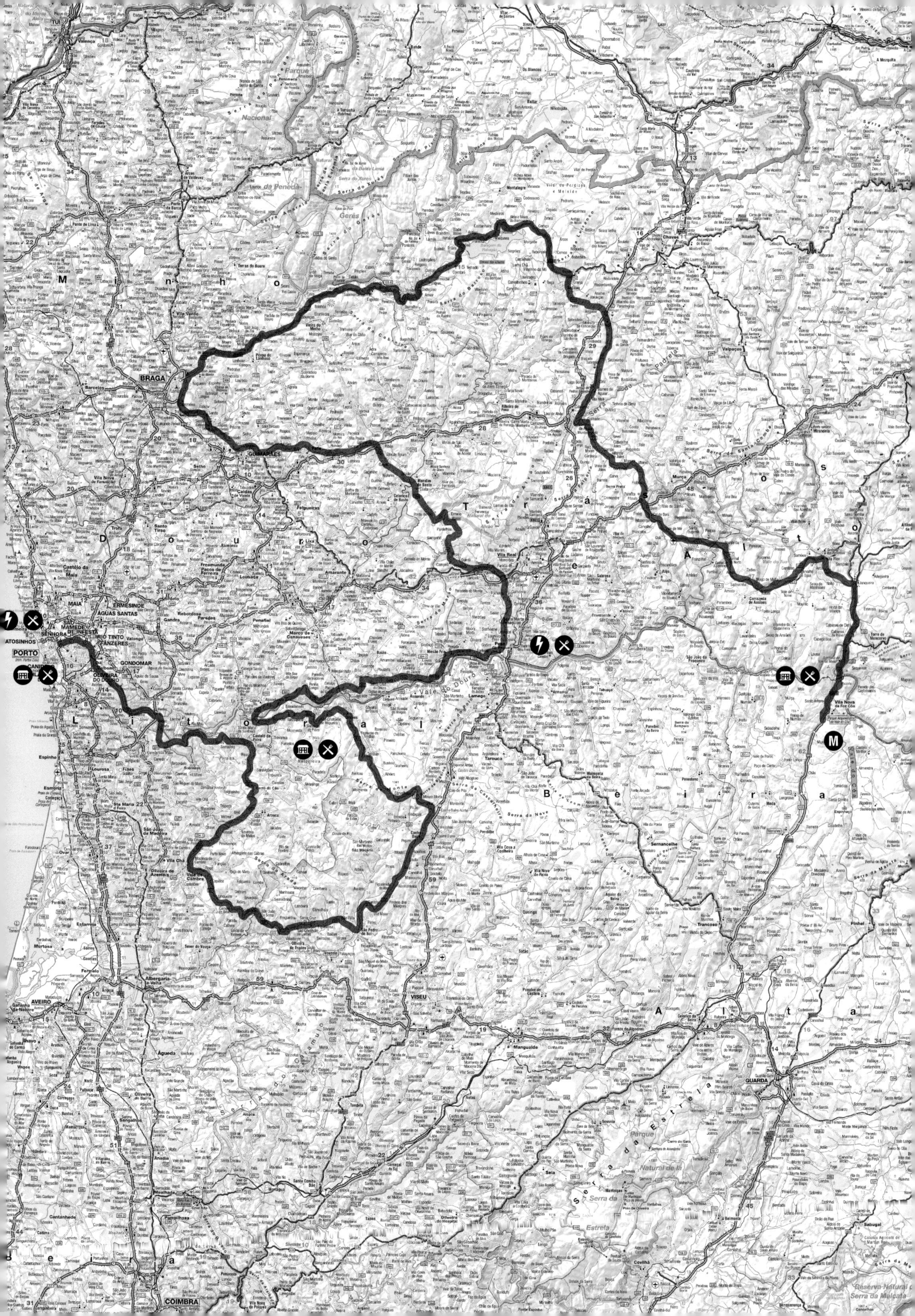

BRAGA
GUIMARÃES
PORTO
MAIA
ERMESINDE
ÁGUAS SANTAS
GONDOMAR
AVEIRO
VISEU
GUARDA
COIMBRA
Chaves
Vila Real
Lamego
Amarante
Felgueiras
Penafiel
Barcelos
Valença
Mangualde
Sever do Vouga
Vale de Cambra
Albergaria-a-Velha
Águeda
Tondela
Trancoso
Pinhel
Sabugal
Covilhã
Belmonte
Seia
Murça
Valpaços
Vila Nova de Foz Côa
Vale do Douro
Serra da Estrela
Serra do Gerês
Minho
Douro Litoral
Trás-os-Montes e Alto Douro
Beira Alta
Reserva Natural da Serra da Malcata

N220

VILA NOVA DE FOZ CÔA MARINHA GRANDE

520 KM • 8 STUNDEN // 324 MILES • 8 HOURS

Die Strapazen der ersten Etappe stecken uns noch in den Knochen, Bilder haben sich uns auf die Netzhäute und ins Gehirn gebrannt: die sich einsam unter einem endlosen Himmel in Hügeln dahinwindende Straße. Und jetzt: Pause. Durchatmen. Die trockene, herbe Atmosphäre im Inneren des Landes aufnehmen. Das muss nach der langen Fahrt von Porto herüber einfach sein.

—

The exertion of the first leg is still in our bones, images have burned themselves onto our retinas and into our brains: The lonesome roads, twisting through hills under an endless sky. And now: pause, take a deep breath. Let the dry, harsh environment of the country's interior sink in. That should be easy after the long drive from Porto.

HOTEL

CASA DAS PENHAS DOURADAS
PENHAS DOURADAS
6260-200 MANTEIGAS
WWW.CASADASPENHASDOURADAS.PT

Aber es geht zu Beginn dieser zweiten Etappe nicht nur um eine Verschnaufpause von der atemlosen Fahrt, sondern auch um eine zweite Reise: Vila Nova de Foz Côa, das ist Wein-Land. Kultur-Land. Altes Land. Menschen, die vor vielen tausend Jahren aus den weiten Räumen im Osten Europas, aus Afrika und Asien hierher gewandert sind und zu den Bewohnern der iberischen Halbinsel wurden, hatten hier ihre Heimat. In den endlosen Hügeln. In den Tälern, den Felsen, den Höhenzügen. Sie haben Spuren hinterlassen, in Stein gefurchte Bilder von Stieren, und sie haben dem Land einen langsamen, unaufhörlichen Schlag verpasst: Die mächtige Zeitlupe uralter Kulturlandschaften.

Erst die Römer konnten hier, am Ende der Welt, einen ersten Tempowechsel herbeiführen – das Imperium rund ums Mittelmeer hat Spanien und Portugal dramatisch verändert. Und die Römer haben den Wein an den Douro gebracht. Zuerst spielte der nur eine untergeordnete und begleitende Rolle, dufte sich vereinzelt an den Flusshängen niederlassen, in den Winkeln von Stützmauern der Hänge. Überdauerte so, zwischen Mandeln und Oliven, die Reiche

But the start of the next stage is not just about taking a breather from the breathless journey; it's also about a second journey: Vila Nova de Foz Côa is wine country. Country with an ancient cultural heritage. Old country. People migrated here many thousands of years ago from the vast expanses of Eastern Europe, Africa and Asia and settled on the Iberian Peninsula, making a home for themselves. In the endless hills.

In the valleys, the rocks, the mountain ranges. They left traces, images of bulls carved in stone, they pounded the land in a slow and steady thud: the mighty slow-motion unfolding of ancient cultural landscapes.

It was the Romans who brought about the first change of pace here at the end of the world – the empire around the Mediterranean has dramatically altered Spain and Portugal. And it was the Romans who brought wine to the Douro. Initially, it played a lesser, underling role, putting down roots here and there in the crannies of the river slopes, in the nooks of the retaining walls. Surviving, between almonds

SERRA DA ESTRELA
NATURAL PARK

SERRA DA ESTRELA
NATURAL PARK

SERRA DA ESTRELA
NATURAL PARK

der Goten und Mauren. Während auf den Ebenen Getreide gezogen wurde – ab dem Mittelalter eines der großen Geschenke Südamerikas: Mais –, ging der Wein in erster Linie an die Klöster und Kirchen. Das Blut Christi.

Während der unfassbaren Ausdehnung des portugiesischen Kolonialreichs im 15., 16. und 17. Jahrhundert saugten immense politische, wirtschaftliche und militärische Anstrengungen das Landesinnere Portugals regelrecht leer, die Bewohner verarmten. Erst die Zweckgemeinschaft Portugals und Englands gegen Spanien änderte diesen Prozess tiefgreifend: Plötzlich wurde portugiesischer Wein das opportune Konkurrenzprodukt zum Wein aus Frankreich, der Handel mit den Engländern nahm Fahrt auf. Olivenöl und Obst wurden schon seit dem 13. Jahrhundert gegen englische Wolle getauscht – nun rückte zusätzlich der Wein ins Interesse der englischen Händler.

Am Douro nahm der Weinanbau zu, um das Jahr 1670 entdeckten englische Händler eine Lösung für das bestimmende Problem des Weins aus dem Süden: Die sonnengeladenen und süßen Reben vom Douro schufen einen auch nach der Vergärung immer noch sehr süßen Wein, der hohe Zuckergehalt führte auf der langen Reise nach England häufig zu seinem Verderben. Zugesetzter Branntwein stoppte nun die Gärung, der hohe Alkoholgehalt und gleichzeitig verbliebener Restzucker machten den Wein aus Portugal haltbar. Auf schmalen Booten mit spitzem Bug und Heck wurden dann die Weinfässer auf dem Douro flussabwärts befördert, bis sie in Porto in den Lagerhallen der großen englischen Kellereien zur weiteren Reifung eingelagert werden konnten. Mit dieser Geschichte kam die Welt ins abgelegene Douro-Tal, eine vollkommen neue Dynamik – aber wer in den Mandelhainen rund um Vila Nova de Foz Côa unterwegs ist, spürt ihn noch: den langsamen Herzschlag dieser Gegend.

Ein letztes Mal fahren wir nach Norden, zurück zur Straße, auf der wir im Verlauf der ersten Etappe angekommen sind, und rollen die N220 entlang zur spanischen

and olives, the kingdoms of the Goths and Moors. While grains were grown on the plains – corn, one of the great gifts from South America from the Middle Ages onwards – most of the wine went to monasteries and churches.

The blood of Christ. During the breathtaking expansion of the Portuguese colonial empire in the 15th, 16th and 17th centuries, immense political, economic and military efforts literally sucked the interior of Portugal dry, impoverishing the people who lived there. It was not until Portugal and England united against Spain that this process changed significantly: Suddenly, Portuguese wine became a lucky rival to French wine, and trade with England gained momentum. Olive oil and fruit had been exchanged for wool from England since the 13th century, now, wine piqued the interest of English traders. Viticulture increased along the Douro.

Around the year 1670, English traders discovered a solution to the dominant issue of wine from the south: the sun-drenched, sweet grapes from the Douro created a wine that was still cloyingly sweet even after fermentation, and the high sugar content often led to the wine spoiling during the long voyage to England. Adding grape spirit stopped the fermentation process, the high alcohol content and residual sugar helped to keep the Portuguese wine from going off. Narrow boats with pointed bow and stern transported the wine barrels downstream on the Douro until they could be stored at Porto in the warehouses of large English wineries to continue the ageing process. With this, the world arrived in the far-flung Douro Valley, bringing with it a completely new dynamic – but anyone exploring the almond groves around Vila Nova de Foz Côa can still feel it: the slow heartbeat of the region.

We sweep to the north one last time, back to the road on which we arrived on leg one. We roll along next to the Douro on the N220 following the Spanish border at the Douro. We treat ourselves to one last glimpse of the river – running narrow and green between the dry slopes of the interior.

HOTEL

CASA DE SÃO LOURENÇO
N232, KM 49.3, 6260-200 MANTEIGAS
WWW.CASADESAOLOURENCO.PT

N232
37

SERRA DA ESTRELA
NATURAL PARK

SERRA DA ESTRELA
NATURAL PARK

SERRA DA ESTRELA
NATURAL PARK

HOTEL

QUINTA DAS LÁGRIMAS
RUA ANTÓNIO AUGUSTO GONÇALVES
COIMBRA, 3041-901
WWW.QUINTADASLAGRIMAS.PT

Grenze am Douro. Wir lassen uns ein letztes Mal mit dem Fluss treiben, der in den trockenen Hängen des Landesinneren schmal und grün unterwegs ist. Dann sagen wir adeus, auf Wiedersehen. Sprinten in südlicher Richtung weg vom Fluss, toben mit der N221 und ihren wilden Windungen davon und landen bald auf einem dürren, weiten Plateau. Nach Süden, immer weiter nach Süden, durch trockene Weiden und steinige Äcker, vorbei an ins Weite geduckten Dörfern, vorbei an knorrigen, vergessenen Klöstern, vorbei an den blockigen Wehrtürmen des Mittelalters. Convento de Santa Maria de Aguiar, Castelo do Pinhel ...

Bei Guarda haben wir den Fuß der Serra da Estrela erreicht, das Gebirge drängt in weitem Bogen nach Süden und wird von schneebedeckten Gipfeln gekrönt, die sich bis auf nahezu 2000 Meter erheben. Mit selbstbewusstem Schwung folgt die Straße eine Weile lang dem Sockel, dann will sie es wissen und bläst hinter Valhelas zum Sturm auf die oberen Stockwerke. Slalom deluxe, auf und zu, links und rechts geht das. Zur Rechten die Gräser am Straßenrand abklatschen und zur Linken über den Mittelstrich räubern oder dicht an Leitplanken entlangzimmern. Immer weiter hastet die Straße hinauf und langsam dämmert einem die schiere Größe des Gebiets. Bei Sabugueiro haben wir die Serra beinahe überquert, setzen aber jetzt erst zum eigentlichen Gipfelsturm an: Von der Westseite geht es zu den kahlen Kuppen hinauf, über die ein kalter Wind faucht, auf denen sich Moose zwischen Geröllmurmeln ducken, während die Straße mit verlorenem Schwung mitten hindurchzieht. So hatten wir uns Portugal nie vorgestellt. Aus den Alpen kennen wir diese steinigen, kalten Höhen – aber das hier ist der sonnige Süden Europas, oder? Ein altbekannter Instinkt

We then say "Adeus" – farewell, sprint away to the south, romp along the N221 with its wild curves and soon arrive at a wide, arid plateau. Pushing south, further and further south, through dry grasslands and stony fields, past crouching villages, gnarled, forgotten monasteries, past the chunky fortified towers of the Middle Ages. Convento de Santa Maria de Aguiar, Castelo do Pinhel...

At Guarda, we reach the foot of the Serra da Estrela, the mountains push to the south in a wide arc and are crowned by snow-covered peaks that tower up to almost 2,000 meters. The road follows the foothills for a while before it's had enough and storms to the upper floors after Valhelas. Slalom Deluxe, opening and closing, left and right. Raking the grass on the right of the road, to the left over the middle line, then a close shave along the guardrails. The road rushes ever upward. Gradually, the sheer size of the area dawns on you. At Sabugueiro, we've almost crossed the Serra, but we're only now starting to make the final ascent to the summit: From the west slope, we reach bare crests, a cold wind howls, mosses hunker between the scree rubble, while the road loses momentum as it passes through. This is not the Portugal we imagined. We only know these stony, chilly altitudes from the Alps – this is Europe's sunny south, isn't it?

An old instinct awakens, lifts its head and shakes off the drowsiness: The pure pleasure of driving. Breathless. Unstoppable. Ever onwards. Avoiding every straight line. We notice how dreadfully addicted we are when we turn at the first crossroads using gut instinct rather than the map. There's something about roads like this: they lure you, promising curves and horror

O seu restaurante

GNR

Ein altbekannter Instinkt blinzelt, hebt den Kopf und schüttelt sich die Schläfrigkeit aus dem Pelz: Die schiere Lust am Fahren. Atemlos. Nicht zu stoppen. Immer weiter. Jede gerade Linie verschmähend. Wir merken, wie grässlich uns diese Sucht erwischt hat, als wir an der ersten Straßenkreuzungen nach Gefühl abbiegen, statt nach Landkarte.

An old instinct awakens, lifts its head and shakes off the drowsiness: The pure pleasure of driving. Breathless. Unstoppable. Ever onwards. Avoiding every straight line. We notice how dreadfully addicted we are when we turn at the first crossroads using gut instinct rather than the map.

blinzelt, hebt den Kopf und schüttelt sich die Schläfrigkeit aus dem Pelz: Die schiere Lust am Fahren. Atemlos. Nicht zu stoppen. Immer weiter. Jede gerade Linie verschmähend. Wir merken, wie grässlich uns diese Sucht erwischt hat, als wir an der ersten Straßenkreuzungen nach Gefühl abbiegen, statt nach Landkarte. Straßen haben so etwas an sich: Sie saugen dich an, versprechen Kurven und Schrecken und Mühsal und du folgst ihnen. Wer einmal den geraden Weg verlassen hat, die Direttissima, wird es immer wieder tun. Und so vergessen wir die Zeit, schnüren wie Straßenköter mit dem Gebirge nach Südwesten, wechseln die Windrichtungen und die Bergflanken. Es ist ein weiter Weg, bis wir bei Ferreira do Zêzere plötzlich aus dem Gebirge heraus sind: Gerade eben noch haben wir den viele Kilometer weit aufgestauten Rio Zêzere überquert und jetzt sind die Berge verschwunden. Wir sind zurück im grünen, weiten Portugal mit seinen weißen Siedlungen, den Feldern, Weiden und Gärten.

Müde fahren wir durch diesen Flickenteppich nach Westen in Richtung Atlantik – und allein der Gedanke ans Meer elektrisiert uns. In Marinha Grande, zehn Kilometer entfernt von der Küste, stranden wir.

and hardship and we can't resist. Anyone who has strayed from the straight and narrow, the Direttissima, will do it again and again. And so we forget the time, rove to the southwest with the mountains like street dogs, changing wind direction and mountainsides. It's a long way before we shake off the mountains at Ferreira do Zêzere: we've just crossed the Rio Zêzere, which has been dammed for many kilometers, and now the mountains disappear. We're back in green, expansive Portugal with its white settlements, fields, pastures and gardens.

Weary, we drive through the patchwork quilt to the west, heading for the Atlantic – and the thought of the ocean alone electrifies us. We strand in Marinha Grande, ten kilometers from the coast. Back in civilization. We stumble upon a small shop that from the outside promises culinary miracles.

SERRA DA ESTRELA NATURAL PARK

Hier muss es sein: Bunte Fischkonserven stapeln sich zu kleinen Türmen in Gelb, Rot, Türkisgrün und Blau, an der Theke serviert die Seniorchefin kleine Wunder zum Probieren: Sardinen mit Zitrone, geräucherte Makrele oder mürbe Stücke vom Kabeljau.

This must be it: rainbow-colored tinned fish are piled into small towers of yellow, red, turquoise green and blue. At the counter, the senior boss offers tiny tantalizing tasters; sardines with lemon, smoked mackerel or tender morsels of cod.

Zurück in der Zivilisation. Wir stolpern in ein kleines Geschäft, das bereits von außen kulinarische Wunder verspricht. Rau und verrucht und fettig, mit älteren Herren, die eine laut klingelnde Tür hinter sich zuziehen, prall gefüllte Tüten und ein zufriedenes Zahnlücken-Grinsen tragen.

Hier muss es sein: Bunte Fischkonserven stapeln sich zu kleinen Türmen in Gelb, Rot, Türkisgrün und Blau, an der Theke serviert die Seniorchefin kleine Wunder zum Probieren: Sardinen mit Zitrone, geräucherte Makrele oder mürbe Stücke vom Kabeljau. Die Leckereien krönen kleine Brotstücke, die sich bereits mit dem Aroma einer kleinen Olivenöl-Pfütze angesteckt haben.

Zumindest am kultivierten Beginn dieser kleinen, kultischen Handlung. Dann muss es mit steigender Gier schneller gehen, es wird gelöffelt, gegabelt, gefingert und gezahnstochert – am Ende lutschen wir öltriefende Finger. Und verlassen das Etablissement durch die laut klingelnde Tür. Mit prall gefüllten Tüten in beiden Händen und einem zufriedenen Grinsen, dem nur die Zahnlücke fehlt.

Rough and wicked and oily, with old gentlemen who pull the door closed behind them with a loud bell jingle, bags full to bursting and wearing a satisfied gap-toothed grin.

This must be it: rainbow-colored tinned fish are piled into small towers of yellow, red, turquoise green and blue. At the counter, the senior boss offers tiny tantalizing tasters; sardines with lemon, smoked mackerel or tender morsels of cod. These delicacies come atop small pieces of bread, infused with the flavor of a small puddle of olive oil.

At least at the cultivated start of the small, ritual act. But then voraciousness takes over, spooned, forked, fingered and toothpicked – until we lick our oil-dripping fingers, and leave the establishment through the loudly ringing door. With bursting bags in both hands and a satisfied grin, with only the gap missing.

HOTEL

VALE D'AZENHA HOTEL & RESIDENCES
R. DA BARRADA 39
2460-342 ALCOBAÇA
WWW.HOTELVALEDAZENHA.COM

VILA NOVA DE FOZ CÔA MARINHA GRANDE

Vom östlichen, trockenen Ende der Weinbaugebiete am Douro starten wir unsere zweite Etappe. Folgen der Straße bis ins Grenzgebiet zwischen Spanien und Portugal, und rollen dann in südlicher Richtung davon, immer in Richtung Guarda. Hier haben wir den Fuß der sogenannten Serra da Estrela erreicht, einem Ausläufer des großen Scheidegebirges im Zentrum der iberischen Halbinsel. Während es die Gipfel auf spanischem Territorium bis auf über 2500 Meter Meereshöhe schaffen, erreicht die Serra da Estrela immerhin noch knapp 2000 Meter und ist damit das höchste Gebirge Portugals. Ein beinahe alpiner Charakter und dünne Besiedlung machen unsere Etappe über den Rücken der Serra zur Herausforderung, die wir inklusive der anschließenden Kilometer in Richtung Coimbra gern annehmen. Bei Lousã drehen wir allerdings bei und schlagen einen Bogen um das Fluss-System des Rio Zêzere, ab Sertã streben wir in Richtung Osten. An Tomar vorüber, über Alburitel und Leiria erreichen wir Marinha Grande – die Küste des Atlantik ist nun nur noch 10 Kilometer entfernt.

—

We begin stage two from the eastern, dry end of the Douro Valley wine region, follow the road to the border of Spain and Portugal, then roll to the south, direction Guarda. Here, we reach the foot of the so-called Serra da Estrela, the foothills of the great dividing range in the centre of the Iberian Peninsula. While the peaks on Spanish territory tower to almost 2,500 meters above sea level, the Serra da Estrela impressively manages just under 2,000 meters and is thus the highest mountain range in Portugal. An almost alpine character and sparse settlements make this stage over the ridge of the Serra somewhat challenging, but that doesn't concern us in the slightest as we head towards Coimbra. At Lousã, however, we heave-to and snake along the river system of the Rio Zêzere. At Sertã, we swing east. Past Tomar, over Alburitel and Leiria, we reach Marinha Grande – the Atlantic coast is now just 10 kilometers away.

520 KM • 8 STUNDEN // 324 MILES • 8 HOURS

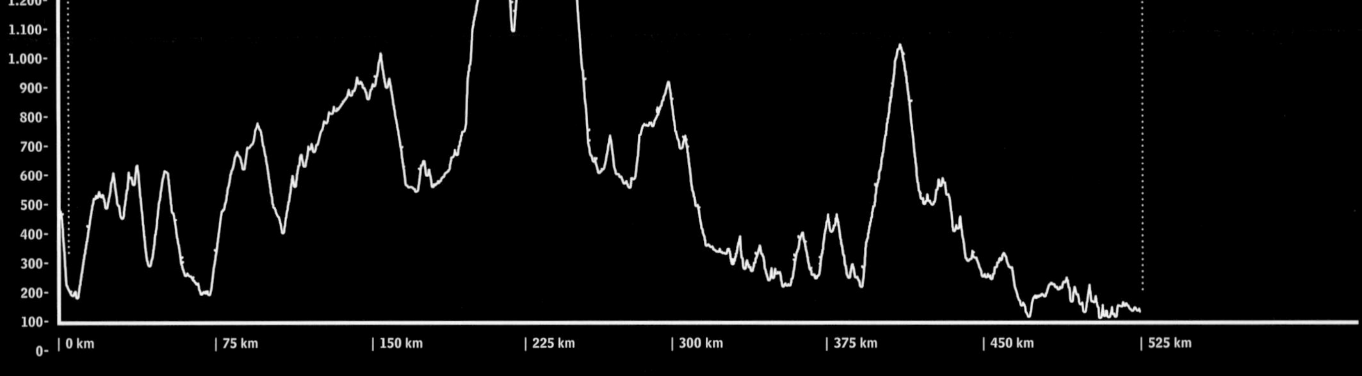

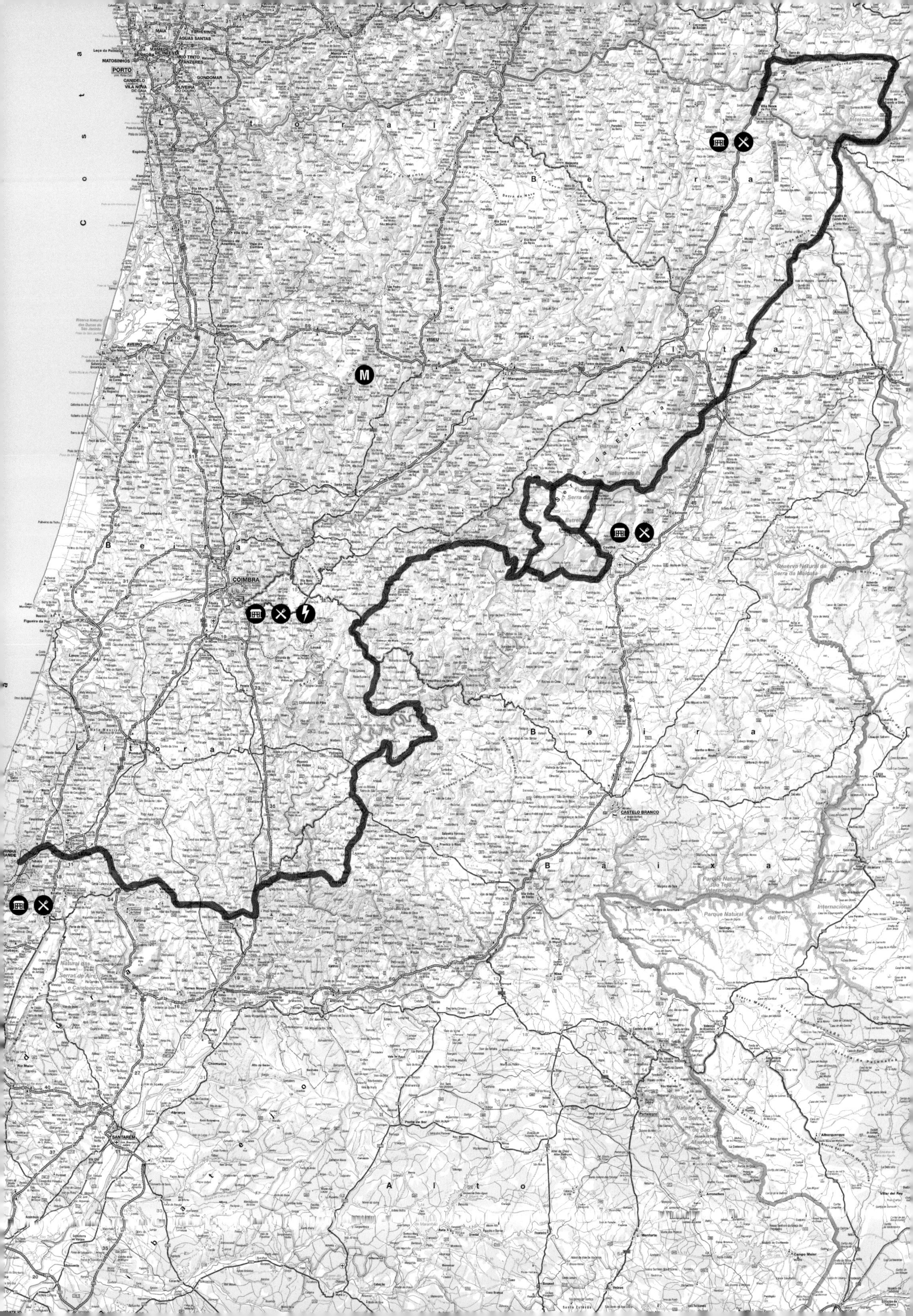

PORTO
AVEIRO
VISEU
COIMBRA
GUARDA
CASTELO BRANCO
SANTARÉM
Mangualde
Trancoso
Pombal
Tomar
Torres Novas
Fundão
Portalegre
Arronches
Campo Maior
Alburquerque
Reserva Natural da Serra da Malcata
Parque Natural do Tejo Internacional
Parque Natural del Tajo Internacional
Parque Natural das Serras de Aire e Candeeiros
Parque Natural da Serra de São Mamede

MARINHA GRANDE LISSABON

270 KM • 6 STUNDEN // 168 MILES • 6 HOURS

Zwischen Porto und Nazaré scheint Gott in Sachen Küstenlinie etwas die Kreativität verlassen zu haben: Lineal angelegt, schnurgerade Linie durchgezogen – bis auf den kurzen Schwenk bei Figueira da Foz, hier muss ein universeller Zwischenfall den Meister kurz abgelenkt haben – und fertig.

—

When designing the coastline between Porto and Nazaré, God seems to have somehow lost his creative knack: simply laid down a ruler and drew a dead-straight line – except for the brief blip at Figueira da Foz, where some universal incident must have distracted the master creator.

Weißer Sand markiert das Land, donnernde Brandung und salzige Luft definieren das Meer. Zumindest scheint das beim Blick auf die Landkarte so einigermaßen plausibel. Spannender wird eine Entdeckungsreise vor Ort. Dann nämlich entdeckst du ein Muster: Die letzten Orte des Festlands liegen nicht an der Atlantikküste, sondern an einem Meer aus Sand, mehrere Kilometer vom Wasser entfernt. Und diese riesige Landschaft aus weißem Sand ist bedeckt von einem endlosen Kiefern-Heer, immer gleichen Bäumen mit roter, schrundiger Rinde und lichter Krone. Stoisch und gelangweilt stehen sie da, schützen sich gegenseitig vor den Winterwinden des Atlantiks und warten im Sommer würzig nach Harz duftend auf das eine oder andere Wildfeuer. Ein Netz von schmalen Wegen portioniert diesen Wald mit seiner immensen Ausdehnung in viele Karos, ansonsten ist das Einerlei der Kiefern auf Sand nur immer wieder unterbrochen, wenn sich ein Fluss oder Bach in wild überwuchertem Bett zum Meer windet. Dort, ganz vorn, verebbt das Kieferndach, wird von Dünen ausgebremst, von Gras und Schilf gestoppt – und dann kommt der Strand. Ein Bilderbuchstrand wie ihn Kinder malen. Oder eben der liebe Gott.

Mit weißem, warmem Sand, in den man seine Zehen graben kann. In dem Myriaden von winzigen Krebslarven sitzen. Der an windigen Tagen zu einem in der Luft grießelnden Element wird, das in den Augen brennt und die Haut kitzelt, in jede Ritze und Falte dringt. Der Wind rast dann Hunderte von Kilometer weit heran, nimmt Salz und Wasserdampf mit sich und reibt dir das genüsslich in die Haare. Während er dabei nach Weite und Tiefe und Abenteuer duftet. Das alles ist in Marinha Grande – einem dieser Orte am Rand des Kiefernmeers – aber noch reine Theorie. Du musst schon losfahren: mit dem Auto, dem Motorrad, dem Fahrrad – Hauptsache mit der Nase im Wind. Denn dann sickert dieses Land über deine Haut und Nüstern erst so richtig an deine Sinne. Wird zu Synapsen-Strom und Gefühl, zu Weisheit und Sehnsucht und Freude.

Irgendwo auf dem schnurgeraden Weg von Marinha zum Wasser hinunter denkst du,

White sand marks the dry land, thundering surf and salt-laden air define the ocean. At least that's what the map indicates. A journey of discovery along the coast is certain to be more exciting – because a pattern emerges: the mainland's outermost towns don't lie on the Atlantic coast, but on a sea of sand several kilometers inland. And this expansive landscape of white sand is covered by an endless army of pines, all the same with red, chapped bark and a light crown. Stoic and bored they stand there, protecting each other from the winter winds blowing in from the Atlantic, and in summer exuding the fragrance of pine resin, waiting for the odd wildfire. A network of narrow trails dissects the immense forest into countless checkered squares, with the monotony of pines on sand only broken by a river or a creek meandering on its wildly overgrown path to the sea. There, at the very front, the pine roof recedes, slowed by the dunes, halted by grasses and reeds – and then the beach. A picture-book beach as children paint it. Or perhaps even God.

White, warm sand to bury your toes in, home to myriads of tiny crab larvae. On windy days, the sand turns into a whirling element, burning the eyes and tickling the skin, finding its way into every crease and crack. The wind races in from hundreds of kilometers away, picking up salt and moisture, rubbing it into your hair with relish – its scent full of breadth and depth and adventure. But all of this is still just theory in Marinha Grande – one of the places on the edge of the sea of pines. You've got to actually get going: by car, motorcycle, pushbike – the main thing is to keep your nose in that wind. Because only this way can the country seep under your skin and into your nostrils and settle in your bones – turning into a sensory-stream and feeling, into wisdom and longing and joy.

Somewhere along that unswerving stretch from Marinha down to the water, you get the idea that the sea of pines bears an uncanny resemblance to an African scrubland savannah – this extravagant uniformity, the heat, the mysterious monotony. You could release elephants here, giraffes and

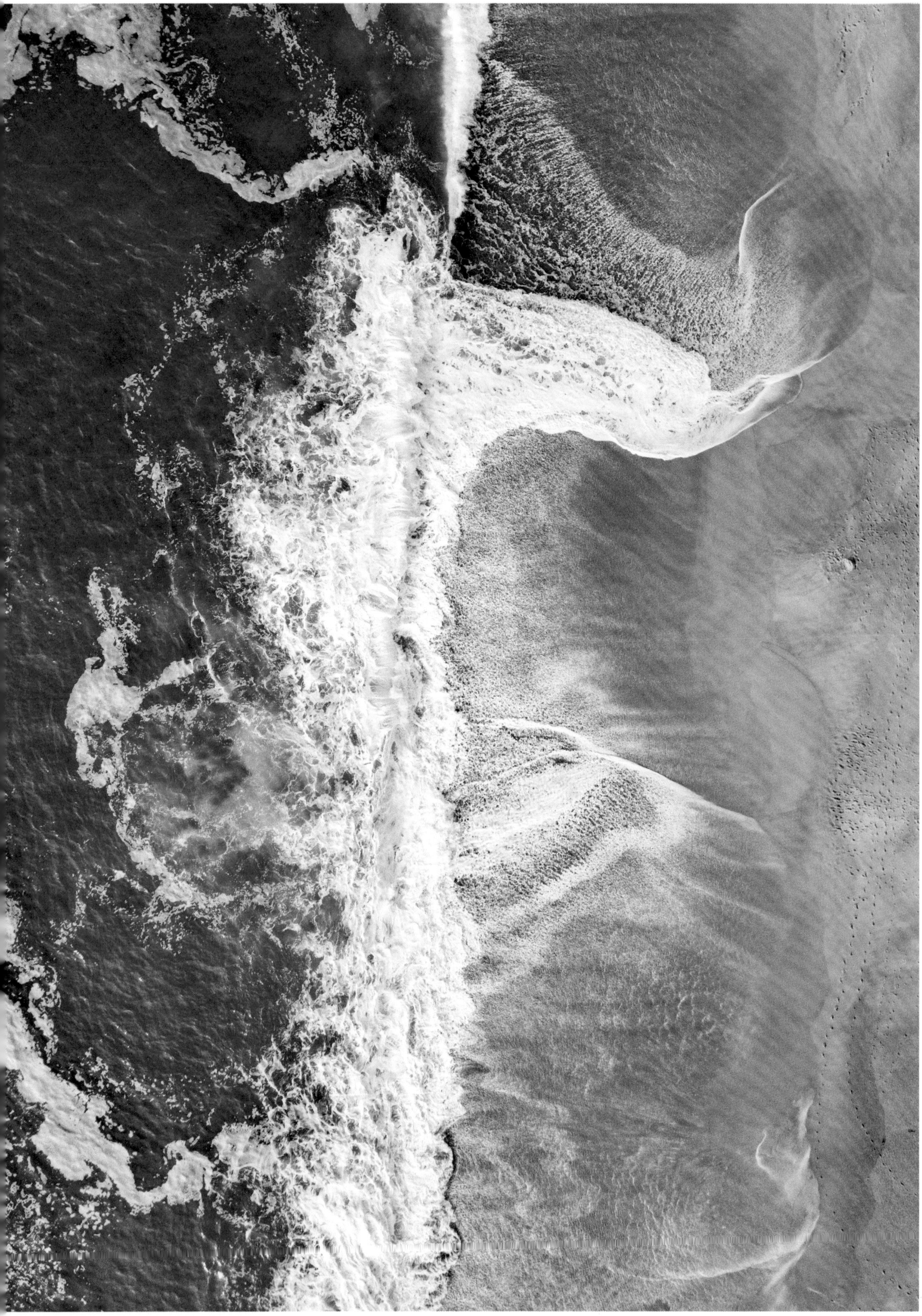

MIRADOURO DAS
AZENHAS DO MAR

dass das Kiefernmeer eine verblüffende Ähnlichkeit mit afrikanischen Strauch-Savannen hat – diese verschwenderische Eintönigkeit, die Hitze, die geheimnisvolle Monotonie. Man könnte hier Elefanten freilassen, Giraffen und Impalas, und sie würden sofort das tun, was Elefanten, Giraffen und Impalas eben so tun, nämlich ganz sie selbst sein, ohne jeden Moment des Fremdelns mit dieser rustikalen Gegend. Genau das passiert aber uns, unten in São Pedro de Moel. Wir bleiben verblüfft stehen, schauen lange aufs Meer hinaus und genießen den unerwarteten Moment innerer Schockstarre: plötzlich Meer. Nach vielen Kilometern im Land, über den Bergen und am Fluss, ist das ein wirklicher Tempowechsel. Das Meer macht etwas mit uns, die klare Grenze der Welten wirkt wie ein Magnet, die Küste zieht magisch an. Plötzlich wird aus den vielen Optionen einer Fahrt durch das Landesinnere nur eine: nach links? Oder nach rechts? – Wir entscheiden uns für links. Nach Süden. In Richtung Lissabon. Aber zuerst: in Richtung Adrenalin.

Das Meer an dieser Küste hat neben endlosen Sandstränden, versteckt hinter Dünen, nämlich auch noch eine ganz andere Seite. Wind und Strömung produzieren entlang der gesamten Küstenlinie immer wieder großartige Wellen, die Surfer aus ganz Europa anziehen – unten in Nazaré herrscht jedoch Ausnahmezustand. Ein riesiger Unterwasser-Canyon vor der Küste lässt die Wellen wie in einem Trichter auf das Land zurasen, sie bäumen sich zu enormer Höhe auf. Aber das ist nicht alles: Durch die Überlappung mit den links und rechts des Kanals in normaler Geschwindigkeit herandrängenden Wassermassen entsteht zusätzliche Dynamik. Turbulenzen. Mehr Wasser, mehr Höhe. Und auch das ist noch nicht das Ende der Geschichte: Eine beinahe parallel zum Strand verlaufende Strömung sorgt für einen regelrechten Turbolader – das Ergebnis ist dann vor allem bei hohem Seegang und auflandigem Wind atemberaubend. Bis zu 30 Meter hohe Wellen wälzen sich in enormem Tempo auf den nördlichen Strand von Nazaré zu und entladen dort, direkt unterhalb des Leuchtturms, ihre brutale Energie. Früher dachte man, die größten Wellen der Erde gäbe es auf Hawaii – inzwischen weiß man es besser:

impalas and they would immediately do what elephants, giraffes and impalas do, namely, be themselves, without feeling at all out of place in this rustic region. And that's precisely what happens to us down in São Pedro de Moel. We stand there mesmerized, gazing out to the ocean, enjoying the unexpected moment of shock and awe: suddenly sea. After many kilometers of land, of mountains and rivers, this truly changes the pace. The ocean does something to us, the clear divide between the worlds is like a magnet, the coast has a magical lure. Suddenly, the many options for driving through the interior of the country narrow down to just one: Left? Right? We choose left. To the south. Towards Lisbon. But first, towards adrenaline.

Aside from the endless beaches, hidden behind dunes, the ocean on this coast has a very different side. Wind and currents regularly produce formidable waves along the entire coastline, which attract surfers from all over Europe. And down at Nazaré, the situation is exceptional. A massive underwater canyon just off the coast causes the waves to pummel towards land as if through a funnel, rearing up to frightening heights. But that's not all. The overlap with water masses moving in at normal speed from the left and right of the channel adds another dynamic. Turbulence. More water, more height. And that's still not the end of the story: A current that runs almost parallel to the beach provides the real turbocharger – and the result is breathtaking, especially with rough seas and an onshore wind. Waves up to 30 meters in height roll with incredible speed towards the northern beach of Nazaré and there discharge their brutal energy just below the lighthouse.

Folks used to think that Hawaii had the biggest waves on Earth – but now they know better: From September, October, when the weather pushes the crazy autumn storms towards the coastline, the world's best big-wave surfers sit in the cafés of Nazaré and wait for the monsters to arrive. Up at the lighthouse, scouts keep an eye out. Down on the beach, teams of surfers and jet-ski sherpas wait. In the cauldrons of the deadly water giants,

HOTEL & RESTAURANT

OUTPOST CASA DAS ARRIBAS
RUA DR. ANTONIO BRANDAO DE VASCONCELOS 35
AZENHAS DO MAR
2705-089 COLARES
WWW.OUTPOST.PT

AT SINTRA

Ab September, Oktober, wenn das Wetter den Irrsinn von Herbststürmen in Richtung Küste drückt, sitzen in den Cafés von Nazaré die weltbesten Big-Wave-Surfer und warten auf den Besuch von Monstern. Oben am Leuchtturm halten Späher Ausschau, unten am Strand warten die Teams aus Surfer und Jetski-Sherpa. Im Hexenkessel der tödlichen Wasserriesen schwimmst du eben nicht einfach mal hinaus um deine Welle zu erwischen. Nur die rohe Power eines Jetski bringt dich an die richtige Position an der Flanke der turmhohen Wasserberge. Von oben sind die gut zu erkennen, meist kommen sie in Serien von drei, vier, fünf Giganten. Dunkles Wasser sammelt sich in der Tiefe und zeigt draußen auf dem Meer

one doesn't simply swim out to catch the wave, it is only the raw power of a jet ski that delivers you to the correct position in the flank of the towering mountains of water. From above, the sets of three, four or five giants are easy to spot. Dark water gathers in the depths and shows its first, mighty humps out at sea, trundling unhindered towards the rocks at Farol da Nazaré. Triggering feelings of fear, trepidation and panic. Then the waves lift their heads, rising higher and higher, inconceivable volumes of gray-blue water. And suddenly, there are these tiny specks in the water, invisible at first from the Cinemascope viewpoint at the lighthouse rock – if they weren't moving as fast as an arrow. Lines

RESTAURANT

RESTAURANTE DA ADRAGA
PRAIA DA ADRAGA, 2710
WWW.RESTAURANTEDAADRAGA.COM

AT SINTRA

erste, mächtige Buckel, die unaufhaltsam auf den Felsen am Farol da Nazaré zukommen. Beängstigend, Gänsehaut und Panikgefühle auslösend. Dann heben die Wellen ihren Kopf, steigen höher und höher, fassungslos machende Mengen von graublauem Wasser. Und plötzlich sind da diese winzigen Punkte im Wasser, die du durch den Cinemascope-Ausblick vom Leuchtturm-Felsen zuerst überhaupt nicht sehen würdest – wenn sie nicht pfeilschnell wären. Linien aus Gischt, die geradewegs auf die sich aufbäumenden Wasserberge zuhalten und genau dann kehrtmachen, wenn die Welle beginnt zu brechen. Der Jetski schießt den Surfer in die Welle, sieht dann zu, dass er sich verdrückt und der Surfer ist jetzt völlig allein da draußen. Wie ein einsamer Bergsteiger in der Felswand. Wird von 500.000 Tonnen Atlantikwasser in Richtung Portugal geprügelt. Glorreich, brandgefährlich, adrenalingepumpt. Und von außen: ein haarsträubendes Schauspiel.

Aufgekratzt fahren wir an der Küste entlang – an der Pilzbucht von Martinho do Porto vorüber, dann will die Lagune von Óbidos umfahren werden und schließlich landen wir am Kap von Peniche. Auch hier wieder: Surfen. Steilküste. Sardinen. Und weiter, wie Fliegende Holländer, die sich vom Wind dahintreiben lassen. Bis zum Cabo da Roca, dem westlichsten Punkt des europäischen Festlands. Möwen surfen über der Klippe, feiner Dunst steigt vom Meer auf, die Luft ist glasig und warm und herrlich. Mittagsblumen haben sich hier überall breitgemacht, fleischige Gäste aus Südafrika, die hier ganz ähnliche Lebensbedingungen vorfinden wie am Kap der Guten Hoffnung.

Der Wind möchte uns weiter über die sandigen Rücken der Küste treiben, aber jetzt widerstehen wir seinem unaufhörlichen Zug. Fahren in die feuchten, grünen Wälder des Sintra-Cascais-Naturparks hinein, auf engen und moosigen Straßen, vorbei am Convento dos Capuchos. So lang, bis wir uns beinahe selbst ganz grün und flechtenbehangen fühlen und in der magischen Bergstadt Sintra angekommen sind. Moos und Flechten und schwarzer Schimmel besiedelt Hauswände, über der Stadt thront als Farbenexplosion der Palácio Nacional da

Der Jetski schießt den Surfer in die Welle, sieht dann zu, dass er sich verdrückt und der Surfer ist jetzt völlig allein da draußen. Wie ein einsamer Bergsteiger in der Felswand. Wird von 500.000 Tonnen Atlantikwasser in Richtung Portugal geprügelt.

A jet ski catapults the surfer into the wave, then makes sure it dashes to safety, leaving the surfer out there completely alone. Like a solo mountain climber on a rock face. Half a million tonnes of water pitching the surfer towards Portugal.

of spray shooting towards the rearing mountains of water, then turning just as the wave begins to break. A jet ski catapults the surfer into the wave, then makes sure it dashes to safety, leaving the surfer out there completely alone. Like a solo mountain climber on a rock face. Half a million tonnes of water pitching the surfer towards Portugal. Glorious, life-threatening, adrenaline-pumped. For onlookers, a hair-raising spectacle.

Exhilarated, we continue along the coast – to the mushroom-shaped bay of Martinho do Porto, sail on past the Óbidos lagoon, before finally landing at the Cape of Peniche. Once again: surfing. Cliffs. Sardines. And onwards, like flying Dutchmen carried on the wings of the wind. To Cabo da Roca, the most westerly point of the European continent. Seagulls surf above the cliff, a fine haze rises from the sea, the air is translucent and warm and wonderful. Midday flowers have spread like a carpet, fleshy guests from South Africa that find living conditions here very similar to those at home at the Cape of Good Hope. The wind wants to carry us further along the sandy ridges of the coastline, but we resist its insistent pull. Instead, we head into the damp, green forests of the Sintra-Cascais Nature Park, on narrow, mossy roads, past the Convento dos Capuchos. Until we arrive in the magical town of Sintra,

HOTEL & RESTAURANT

FAROL HOTEL
AV. REI HUMBERTO II DE ITALIA 7
2750-800 CASCAIS
WWW.FAROL.COM.PT

RESTAURANTE PORTO SANTA MARIA
ESTRADA DO GUINCHO
2750-642 CASCAIS

AT SINTRA

Pena und will unbedingt studiert werden. Auch die Gärten dahinter, mit ihren riesigen Steinen und dem verwunschenen Dickicht, erweisen sich als Magnete und am Castelo dos Mouros geht uns jeder Wille zur Weiterfahrt aus. Wir sind verwunschen, auf ewig gefangen in der melancholischen Schönheit dieser Welt.

Aber dann kommt dieser Windstoß, kalt und scharf, der uns wieder auf die Straße treibt. Bis Linhó und dort auf der N9-1 durch den Korkwald hinunter an den Praia do Guincho. Einen Strand voller Rauheit und Schönheit, der uns auch auf den nächsten Kilometern bis Cascais begleitet: Sanddünen mogeln sich auf die Straße, Klippen ragen über dem Meer auf und immer wieder haben sich Fischrestaurants angesiedelt, die mit Blicken in den Sonnenuntergang locken. Dass die Stadt nicht mehr weit ist, wird nun ebenfalls klar: Auf dem Weg neben der Straße am Meer wird geradelt und gejoggt, der Verkehr nimmt zu, das Leben hat eben seine eigene Brandung. Und sie will gesurft werden: Wir werfen uns ins Gewühl, rollen durch Cascais, umgehen Estoril und dann sind wir nach vielen Kilometern zwischen Stadt und Meer am Torre de Belém gelandet. Dem Tor nach Lissabon.

ourselves feeling almost completely green and moss-covered. Moss and lichen and black mold live on the house walls. Palácio Nacional da Pena towering above the city in an explosion of color convinces us to stop and explore. Behind it, the gardens with massive boulders and the enchanted thicket prove irresistible and at Castelo dos Mouros we run out of will to continue. We are bewitched, forever caught in the melancholy beauty of this world.

But then comes a gust of wind, cold and piercing, propelling us back to the road. To Linhó and there onto the N9-1 through the cork forest down to Praia do Guincho. To a beach of raw beauty, which accompanies us for the next few kilometers to Cascais: sand dunes creep over the streets, cliffs loom above the ocean and fish restaurants with stunning sunset views line up along the coastline. Obviously, the city isn't far away: on the path between the road and the ocean, people cycle and jog, traffic is heavier, life has a different flow. And it wants to be surfed: We throw ourselves into the crush, roll through Cascais, bypass Estoril, and after a few kilometers, end up sandwiched between city and sea at Torre de Belém. The gateway to Lisbon.

HOTEL & RESTAURANT

THE LISBOANS
TRAVESSA DO ALMADA, 9
1100-018 LISBOA, PORTUGAL
WWW.THELISBOANS.COM

CABO DA ROCA

MARINHA GRANDE LISSABON

Die Route der dritten Etappe wird vom Meer definiert. Vergessen sind die Berge des Landesinneren – jetzt hat der Atlantik das Sagen. Auf häufig schnurgeraden Straßen rollen wir parallel zur Küstenlinie, es sind die kleinen Fischer- und Bade-Dörfer, die uns immer wieder ans Meer locken, um dort auf den breiten, weißen Stränden das Hochgefühl eines Tags am Meer zu genießen. Aber auch die Klippen und Riffe haben es in sich: In Nazaré sind mit etwas Wetterglück die höchsten Wellen der Erde zu beobachten, die von einer Big-Wave-Surfer-Elite bezwungen werden – oder auch umgekehrt. Und ein paar Kilometer weiter liegt am Cabo da Roca der westlichste Punkt des europäischen Festlands. Mit dem Sintra-Cascais-Naturpark bietet die dritte Etappe ein fantastisches Kontrastprogramm zu den Kilometern am Meer: In schroffen Bergen voller dichtem Grün sammelt sich die Luftfeuchte des Atlantiks und erschafft so eine magische Welt, die mit ihren Schlössern, Klöstern und Mauren-Burgen unbedingt erkundet werden will. In Cascais hat uns dann das Meer wieder – und wir beinahe das Ziel erreicht: Lissabon, die Hauptstadt Portugals wartet auf uns.

—

The route of the third stage is characterized by the sea. The inland mountains are forgotten, now the Atlantic is in charge. On straight-as-a-die roads we follow the coastline, enjoying the small fishing and seaside villages that constantly beckon to us to come and savor a day at the wide, white beaches. But the cliffs and reefs are also hard to resist. With a bit of luck with the weather, you can watch how the world's best big-wave surfers conquer the highest waves on Earth – or vice versa. Cabo da Roca several kilometers further on is the westernmost point of mainland Europe. Thanks to the Sintra-Cascais Nature Park, leg three offers a fantastic contrast program to the many kilometers of ocean: The humidity of the Atlantic gathers in the rugged hills full of dense foliage, creating a magical world that is irresistible with its castles, monasteries and Moorish fortresses. We meet the ocean again at Cascais – and we've almost reached our destination: Lisbon, Portugal's capital awaits us.

270 KM • 6 STUNDEN // 168 MILES • 6 HOURS

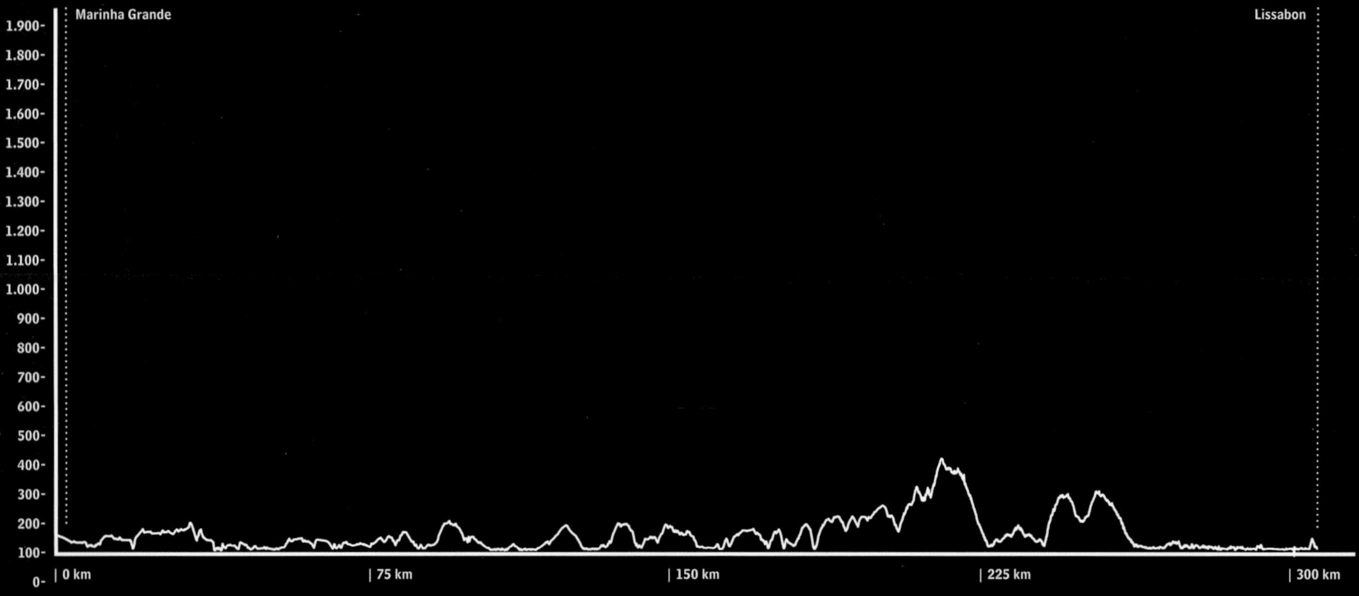

CURVES
— MAGAZIN EST. 2011 —
soulful driving

Costa de Prata
Litoral
Estremadura
Ribatejo
Reserva Natural
Farilhões
Forcadas
das Berlengas
Oceano
Estelas
Berlenga
Cabo Carvoeiro
Peniche
Nazaré
MARINHA GRANDE
LEIRIA
Batalha
Pombal
Vila Nova de Ourém
Fátima
Tomar
Torres Novas
Entroncamento
Golegã
Chamusca
Alcobaça
Porto de Mós
Parque Natural das Serras de Aire e Candeeiros
Alcanena
CALDAS DA RAINHA
Óbidos
Rio Maior
SANTARÉM
Almeirim
Alpiarça
Cartaxo
Bombarral
Cadaval
Lourinhã
TORRES VEDRAS
Alenquer
Azambuja
Benavente
Mafra
Ericeira
SINTRA
ALGUEIRÃO
CACÉM
RIO DE MOURO
QUELUZ
AMADORA
ODIVELAS
LOURES
ALCABIDECHE
CARNAXIDE
SÃO DOMINGOS DE RANA
CASCAIS
Estoril
PAÇO DE ARCOS
OEIRAS
Belém
LISBOA
Sacavém
ALVERCA DO RIBATEJO
PÓVOA DE SANTA IRIA
Vila Franca de Xira
Reserva Natural do Estuário do Tejo
MONTIJO
ALMADA
BARREIRO
CORROIOS
AMORA
ARRENTELA
Seixal
Costa da Caparica
CHARNECA da Caparica
Palmela
Coruche
Vendas Novas

ATM

LISSABON SAGRES

400 KM • 6,5 STUNDEN // 249 MILES • 6,5 HOURS

Ach, Lissabon. Du hast uns fest in deinem Griff. Wie du dich über sieben Hügel weit in die Bucht des Tejo schmiegst, wie hell und bunt du bist. Mit den Farben der Graffiti – sich transformierenden Blumen, schwirrenden Kolibri, straßenzugweit dahinwandernden Comic-Helden-Umzügen, flackernden Kristall-Explosionen und traurig dreinschauenden Schönheiten, alle fassadengroß und so wunderschön.

—

Oh, Lisbon. You have captured our heart. How you hug the seven hills far into the bay of the Tejo, how bright and colorful you are. Embellished with graffiti – transforming flowers, whirring hummingbirds, comic-hero processions parading along the length of the street, flickering crystal explosions and beauties with a sorrowful look in their eyes, all the size of facades and utterly beautiful.

HOTEL & RESTAURANT

SANTA CLARA
CAMPO DE SANTA CLARA
128 1100-473 LISBOA
WWW.SILENTLIVING.PT

ELEVEN RESTAURANT
RUA MARQUÊS DE FRONTEIRA
JARDIM AMÁLIA RODRIGUES
1070 LISBOA
WWW.RESTAURANTELEVEN.COM

JNCQUOI
AV. LIBERDADE 182-184
1250-146 LISBOA
WWW.JNCQUOI.COM

JNCQUOI ASIA
AV. LIBERDADE 144
1250-146 LISBOA
WWW.JNCQUOI.COM

Mit dem Glanz der Azulejos, den fein bemalten Kacheln und ihren bunten Mustern. Und mit der freundlichen Umarmung der Sonne am azurblauen Himmel. Wir planschen durch die Brunnen am Oceanário, wir ziehen durch die Gassen der Altstadt, lassen uns vom Schaukeln der Straßenbahnwagen einlullen, vom Elevador de Santa Justa auf ein ganz neues Niveau heben und irgendwann haben wir selbst die schmale Treppe hinauf zur Aussichtsplattform des Arco da Rua Augusta-Triumphbogens gefunden. Dort stehen wir dann seufzend, mit einem Blick über die Dächer der Stadt, und sind uns wirklich nicht sicher, ob man Lissabon jemals wieder verlassen kann, ohne einen Widerhaken all dieser Schönheit zurückzubehalten. Der Fado Lissabons, in Gesang gegossener Weltschmerz, hat anscheinend schon irreversible Spuren bei uns hinterlassen.

Aber das ist uns dann irgendwie doch zu viel Pathos im Überschwang des Moments. Zurück zu den einfachen Freuden. Zurück zu den Pasteis de Belém oder auch: Pastel de Nata. Diesen mit gezuckertem Eigelb gefüllten Blätterteigtörtchen, die goldgelb, crisp und mit einem Hauch von Backofen-Sonnenbrand in den Auslagen der Bäckereien arme Seelen anlocken, die dann nie wieder einen Ausweg aus der Pasteis-Sucht finden. Zugegeben: Man könnte versuchen, den Pasteis-Kreislauf mit einer regelmäßigen Dosis des Sauerkirschlikörs „Ginja" zu durchbrechen. Aber das gehen täglich viele Lissaboner genauso an – Erfolge sind nicht bekannt. Man munkelt sogar, die Ginja-Abhängigkeit sei ebenso streng und süß, wie die von den Blätterteig-Teufelchen. Wer sich dann endgültig im zuckrigen Verhängnis Portugals verstrickt hat, wird darüber hinaus mit großer Wahrscheinlichkeit zur leichten Beute des „Molotoff". Kein Cocktail, keine Brandbombe ... das heißt, beinahe: Um den Molotoff herzustellen, wird eine Menge Eiweiß und Zucker in einen Aggregatzustand verwandelt, den man in Frankreich Meringue nennen würde, danach darf

With the luster of the Azulejos, the intricately painted tiles and their colorful patterns. We splash around the pools at the Oceanário, stroll through the lanes of the old town, allow ourselves to be lulled by the rocking of the trams, lifted to a whole new level by the Elevador de Santa Justa and, at some point, we find ourselves on the narrow stairs leading up to the viewing platform of the Arco da Rua Augusta triumphal arch. There, we stand and sigh. Gazing at the view over the roofs of the city, we begin to wonder if we can ever leave Lisbon, while all this beauty holds us back like a hook. Lisbon's Fado, weltschmerz poured into song, has obviously left its indelible marks on us.

But there's somehow too much pathos for us in the exuberance of this moment. Back to simple joys. Back to the Pasteis de Belém or the Pastel de Nata. These puff pastry tartlets, filled with su-gary, golden-yellow custard, crisp and lightly tanned in the oven on display in bakery windows, entice poor souls, who then never find a way out of the Pasteis addiction. Admittedly, one could try to break the Pasteis cycle with a regular dose of the sour cherry liqueur "Ginja". But many natives of Lisbon do exactly this every day – apparently without much success. Rumor has it that the Ginja addiction is just as severe and sweet as the tartlet devils. Those who become obsessed with Portugal's propensity for sugar will very likely also fall prey to the "Molotoff". No, not the cocktail and not the incendiary bomb... but almost: To make the Molotoff, a mountain of protein and sugar is whipped into a meringue. The stiff, sugary egg-white mass is then dolloped into a baking tin, drenched in caramel sauce and popped in the oven. What emerges is a crunchy, fluffy sensation. A bomb, indeed.

Imminent tooth loss and sugar shock? Perhaps switch to something a little more savory? We still have some canned fish on offer. They're also here on the shelves in

LISSABON

70

PRAIA DE MONTE CLÉRIGO

Ein Fisch, der überhaupt nicht in portugiesischen Gewässern vorkommt, für den die Portugiesen aber eine echte Schwäche haben, nach Jahrzehnten und Jahrhunderten der Kabeljau-Liebe vielleicht sogar ein Kabeljau-Gen.

die steife Masse in eine mit Karamellsoße imprägnierte Backform schlüpfen und sich im Backofen zu einer knackig-fluffigen Sensation verwandeln lassen. Bombe, also doch.

Drohender Zahnausfall und Zuckerschock? Lieber wieder zu etwas Pikantem wechseln? – Wir hätten da ja noch ein paar Fischkonserven im Angebot. Auch in Lissabon findet man sie in den Regalen, flache Dosen in bunten Nostalgie-Schächtelchen und darin in Öl badend die feinsten Sardinen- oder Thunfisch-Stücke, aromatisiert mit Knoblauch, Zitrone und anderen Leckereien. Und wer dann vom moderaten Thun über die fortgeschritten fischige Sardine bis zur ungeheuerlich fettigen und gehaltvollen Makrele vorgestoßen ist, nimmt es sogar mit dem Bacalhau auf, dem Kabeljau. Ein Fisch, der überhaupt nicht in portugiesischen Gewässern vorkommt, für den die Portugiesen aber eine echte Schwäche haben, nach Jahrzehnten und Jahrhunderten der Kabeljau-Liebe vielleicht sogar ein Kabeljau-Gen.

Dass hinten an der Fischtheke Bacalhau verkauft wird, riechst du bereits am Eingang der Läden und wenn du als Anfänger das erste Mal die getrockneten, gesalzenen Fischkadaver siehst, möchtest du lieber kein Fortgeschrittener werden. Aber das gehört zu den vermutlich gröbsten, menschenmöglichen Fehleinschätzungen. Denn sobald man die staubtrockenen Kabeljau-Filets wässert, verwandeln sie sich in etwas ganz augenscheinlich Essbares. Und nicht nur das: Frittiert oder in Pasteten und Törtchen ist der reanimierte Bacalhau eine zartfeste, luftig-leichte Köstlichkeit. Und zu Recht Portugals Leib- und Magenspeise. Versöhnt mit der Welt, verliebt in Lissabon

A fish that is not found in Portuguese waters, but for which the Portuguese have a real soft spot. After decades and centuries of love for cod, perhaps they've developed a cod gene.

Lisbon, flat tins in colorful nostalgic packaging, containing the finest morsels of sardine or tuna, bathed in oil and flavored with garlic, lemon and other delicacies. And those who have progressed from moderate tuna to the very fishy sardines and on to the incredibly oily and rich mackerel could even try out the bacalhau. Cod. A fish that is not found in Portuguese waters, but for which the Portuguese have a real soft spot. After decades and centuries of love for cod, perhaps they've developed a cod gene. The minute you walk into a shop, you can smell that bacalhau is sold at the fish counter.

When you see the dried, salted fish carcasses for the first time as a rookie, your first instinct will be to remain a neophyte – however, this could be one of the greatest misjudgments known to mankind. Because, as soon as water is added to the bone-dry cod fillets, they turn into something very obviously edible. And not only that: fried or added to pies and tarts, the reanimated bacalhau becomes a tender, light and airy delicacy. And justifiably one of Portugal's all-time favorites.

Reconciled with the world, in love with Lisbon, and above all, completely sated, we leave the city. In style, of course, over the Ponte 25 de Abril, which looks like the Golden Gate Bridge and makes every effort to give the start of the next leg a San Francisco

HOTEL & RESTAURANT

SPATIA COMPORTA
N261-1, ESTRADA DAS BICAS
MARCO DA SAIBREIRA, BICAS
7570-337 GRÂNDOLA
WWW.SPATIACOMPORTA.COM

SUBLIME COMPORTA -
COUNTRY RETREAT & SPA
EN 261-1, MUDA, CCI 3954
7570-337 GRÂNDOLA
WWW.SUBLIMECOMPORTA.PT

HOTEL & RESTAURANT

TRÊS MARIAS
7645-909 VILA NOVA DE MILFONTES
WWW.TRES-MARIAS-PT.BOOK.DIRECT/DE-DE

und vor allem pappsatt verlassen wir die Stadt. Natürlich stilecht über die Ponte 25 de Abril, die aussieht wie die Golden Gate Bridge und die sich beim Überqueren auch sonst alle Mühe gibt, dem Etappen-Start ein Gefühl von San Francisco zu verleihen: Unter uns zieht der Rio Tejo zum Atlantik, zur Linken wirkt die Bucht der Flussmündung tatsächlich wie die Bucht von San Francisco und erst die Christus-Statue am anderen Ufer zerstört den Kalifornien-Moment mit einem Rio-de-Janeiro-Schocker. Für ein paar Kilometer bleiben wir jetzt auf der A2 in Richtung Süden, wechseln dann zur N378 nach Sesimbra und drehen kurz vor der kleinen Küstenstadt ab: in das Bergmassiv der Serra da Arrábida an der Küste, auf die M525 und dann immer der Nase nach.

Oder besser gesagt, dem Verlauf der Serra folgend. Das Küstengebirge zwischen Sesimbra und Setúbal ist herrlich wild und rau, schmal und gierig wieselt die Straße dahin, transformiert sich in groovende Kilometer. Als N379-1 ist sie direkt am Klippenhang gelandet und hat einen ganz großen Auftritt. Aus erhabener Höhe staunen wir zur darunter liegenden Bucht hinab, die türkisgrün und blau zwischen dem Steilhang der Serra da Arrábida und der Halbinsel Troia auf der anderen Seite liegt. Grobschlächtige Kalkfels-Köpfe ragen aus der Macchia, Kermeseichen, Johannisbrotbäume oder Lorbeer klammern sich an die Hänge. Felswände zur Linken, das weite Meer zur Rechten, so surfen wir in Aussichtslage dahin und nähern uns mit jedem Bergrücken dem nächsten Zwischenziel.

Bis Setúbal rollen wir, und schaffen es dann gerade noch auf die Fähre, die über die Mündung des Rio Sado von Setúbal hinüber zur Halbinsel Troia fährt. Gelassen stampft der Stahlkoloss in Grün und Rot übers Wasser und wenn wir Glück hätten, würden jetzt auch noch die Delfine auftauchen,

feeling: Below us, the Rio Tejo flows to the Atlantic, to the left, the bay of the estuary indeed resembles San Francisco Bay. Only the Statue of Christ on the opposite shore disturbs the Californian moment with a Rio de Janeiro shock. We stay on the A2 to the south for a few kilometers then switch to the N378 to Sesimbra, taking the turn-off just before the small coastal town.

Into the Serra da Arrábida mountain range at the coast, then join the M525 and from there just follow our nose. Or rather, follow the course of the Serra. The coastal mountains between Sesimbra and Setúbal are gloriously wild and rugged, the road scurries narrow and voracious, transforming into rhythmic kilometers. As the N379-1, it lands directly on the cliff slope and affords us a magnificent vista. From this lofty height, we marvel at the bay below – turquoise green and blue between the steep slope of the Serra da Arrábida and the Troia Peninsula on the other side. Rugged limestone outcrops loom out of the shrubland, kermes oak, carob trees and laurel cling to the slopes. Cliffs to the left, the open ocean to the right – that's how we surf along, panorama-style, as we head, ridge by ridge, to our next stopover.

We continue as far as Setúbal, just in time to catch the ferry, which takes us across the mouth of the Rio Sado from Setúbal to the Troia Peninsula. The green-and-red steel behemoth calmly ploughs through the water. If we're lucky, we'll spot the dolphins that live between the river mouth and the Atlantic bay. It's supposed to be a whole pod and we scan the water, squinting as the sun glistens on the surface, alas without luck. At least not when it comes to dolphins. But definitely in every other respect. Because from Grândola we begin a majestic stage along the west coast. Comporta, Melides, Sines. Here, we take a break

PRAIA DE BODEIRA

PRAIA DE CORDOAMA

CABO DE SÃO VICENTE

Nur die Statue von Vasco da Gama, dem wohl berühmtesten Sohn der Stadt und Entdecker des Seewegs nach Indien, harrt bewegungslos auf ihrem Sockel aus und späht zum Horizont, als würden dort jeden Moment wieder verschollene Schiffe der kolonialen Hoch-Zeiten Portugals erscheinen.

die zwischen Flussmündung und Atlantikbucht leben. Eine ganze Schule soll es sein und wir suchen die in der Sonne glitzernde Wasseroberfläche mit den Augen ab, haben aber kein Glück. Zumindest nicht in Delfin-Angelegenheiten.

In jeder sonstigen Hinsicht aber ganz bestimmt. Denn ab Grândola starten wir in eine königliche Etappe entlang der Westküste. Comporta, Melides, Sines. Hier legen wir einen kurzen Zwischenstopp ein, tasten uns durch die schmalen Gassen des Städtchens bis zum Hafen. Im Schatten weißblauer Häuser rumpelt Kopfsteinpflaster, die Hitze des Nachmittags verordnet dem Leben eine kurze Zwangspause. Nur die Statue von Vasco da Gama, dem wohl berühmtesten Sohn der Stadt und Entdecker des Seewegs nach Indien, harrt bewegungslos auf ihrem Sockel aus und späht zum Horizont, als würden dort jeden Moment wieder verschollene Schiffe der kolonialen Hoch-Zeiten Portugals erscheinen.

Bei Vila Nova de Milfontes geht es über den Rio Mira, der in seinem grünen Tal kurz noch einmal Erinnerungen an den Douro aufkommen lässt. Und hinter São Teotónio wacht die Straße dann tatsächlich noch einmal aus ihrem schläfrigen Küsten-Trab auf, sie wird für einige Kilometer wieder spannend und lebendig. Die Temperaments-Aufwallung ist allerdings schnell vorüber, es geht in entspanntem Rhythmus weiter nach Süden. Zwischen Aljezur und Vila do Bispo steht dann erneut Kurven-Swing auf dem Programm – acht Kilometer später, am Leuchtturm des Cabo de São Vicente, haben wir das Ziel erreicht: Der äußerste Südwesten Portugals, von hier aus geht es nur in östlicher Richtung weiter.

Only the statue of Vasco da Gama, probably the most famous son of the town and discoverer of the sea route to India, remains motionless on its pedestal and scans the horizon as if waiting for the ships of Portugal's lost colonial heyday to appear at any moment.

and wander through the narrow lanes of the small town to the harbor. Cobblestones stumble in the shade of houses painted white and blue, the afternoon heat has driven life indoors for a short siesta. Only the statue of Vasco da Gama, probably the most famous son of the town and discoverer of the sea route to India, remains motionless on its pedestal and scans the horizon as if waiting for the ships of Portugal's lost colonial heyday to appear at any moment.

At Vila Nova de Milfontes we cross the Rio Mira, which, with its green valley, brings back memories of the Douro. After São Teotónio, the road wakes up again from its sleepy coastal trot, once more lively and invigorated for a few kilometers. The mood lift, however, soon disappears, and the rhythm relaxes again as we head further south. Between Aljezur and Vila do Bispo the twisty road returns – eight kilometers later, at the Cabo de São Vicente lighthouse, we reach our destination: the most south-westerly point of Portugal. From here, there's only one way forward: East.

HOTEL & RESTAURANT

MARTINHAL SAGRES BEACH FAMILY RESORT HOTEL
R. BAIONA LA REAL APARTADO 54
8650-908 SAGRES
WWW.MARTINHAL.COM/SAGRES/DE

LISSABON SAGRES

Lissabon zieht mit seiner Dynamik, Schönheit und Geschichte Besucher aus der ganzen Welt an, die Hauptstadt Portugals mit ihren rund 500.000 Einwohnern ist Startpunkt unserer Etappe. Ohne eine intensive Begegnung mit dieser Stadt ist eine Portugal-Reise kaum denkbar, es lohnt sich, hier auch mehrere Tage einzuplanen. Auf der weiteren Fahrt nach Süden rollen wir über die Halbinsel im Süden und hinein ins Küstengebirge Serra da Arrábida. Dieser Bogen sollte keinesfalls ausgelassen werden, die unter Naturschutz stehende Landschaft ist wunderschön und bietet majestätische Ausblicke auf die Bucht an der Mündung des Rio Sado. Hinter Setúbal macht die Route nach Süden zwei Vorschläge: Entweder umrundet man die Mündung des Sado-Flusses in einem weiten Bogen nach Osten, wer sich jedoch Zeit nimmt, hat mit der Fährfahrt zur vorgelagerten Halbinsel Troia und einer Fortsetzung der Fahrt dicht am Atlantik die landschaftlich eindeutig schönere Wahl getroffen. In Sines statten wir der Geburtsstadt des portugiesischen Seefahrers und Entdeckers Vasco da Gama einen Besuch ab, danach sind wir am Rand des Naturparks Alentejano unterwegs, der bis zur Südwestspitze der iberischen Halbinsel bei Sagres führt.

—

Lisbon lures visitors from all over the world with its dynamism, beauty and history. The capital of Portugal with its 500,000 or so inhabitants is the starting point for our next leg. A trip to Portugal would be unthinkable without spending a decent amount of time exploring the city. Best to set aside a couple of day for this. On the drive to the south, we roll over the peninsula and into the Serra da Arrábida range. This arc is a must, the protected landscape is stunning and offers majestic views of the bay at the mouth of the Rio Sado. After Setúbal, there are two routes to the south: Either circling the mouth of the Sado River in a wide arc to the east, or, if you have time, catch the ferry to the Troia Peninsula and continue the journey close to the Atlantic. Obviously, the more beautiful option. At Sines, we pay a visit to the birthplace of the Portuguese navigator and explorer Vasco da Gama, then head to the edge of the Alentejano Natural Park, which leads to the south-westerly tip of the Iberian Peninsula near Sagres.

400 KM • 6,5 STUNDEN // 249 MILES • 6,5 HOURS

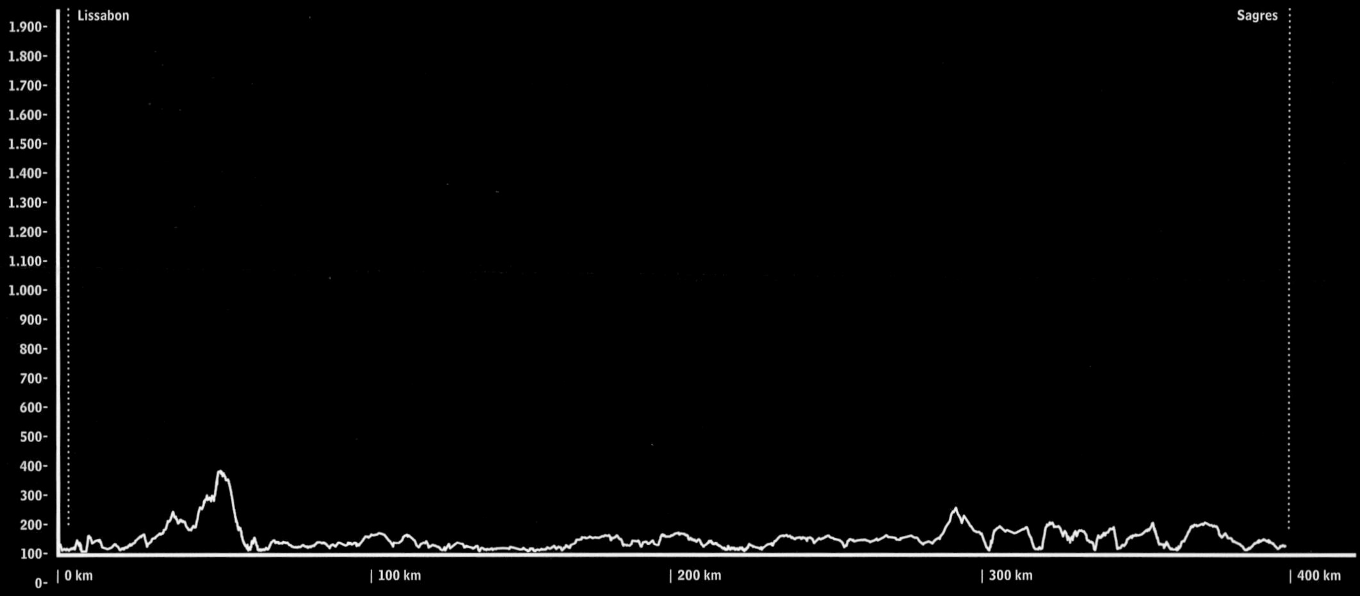

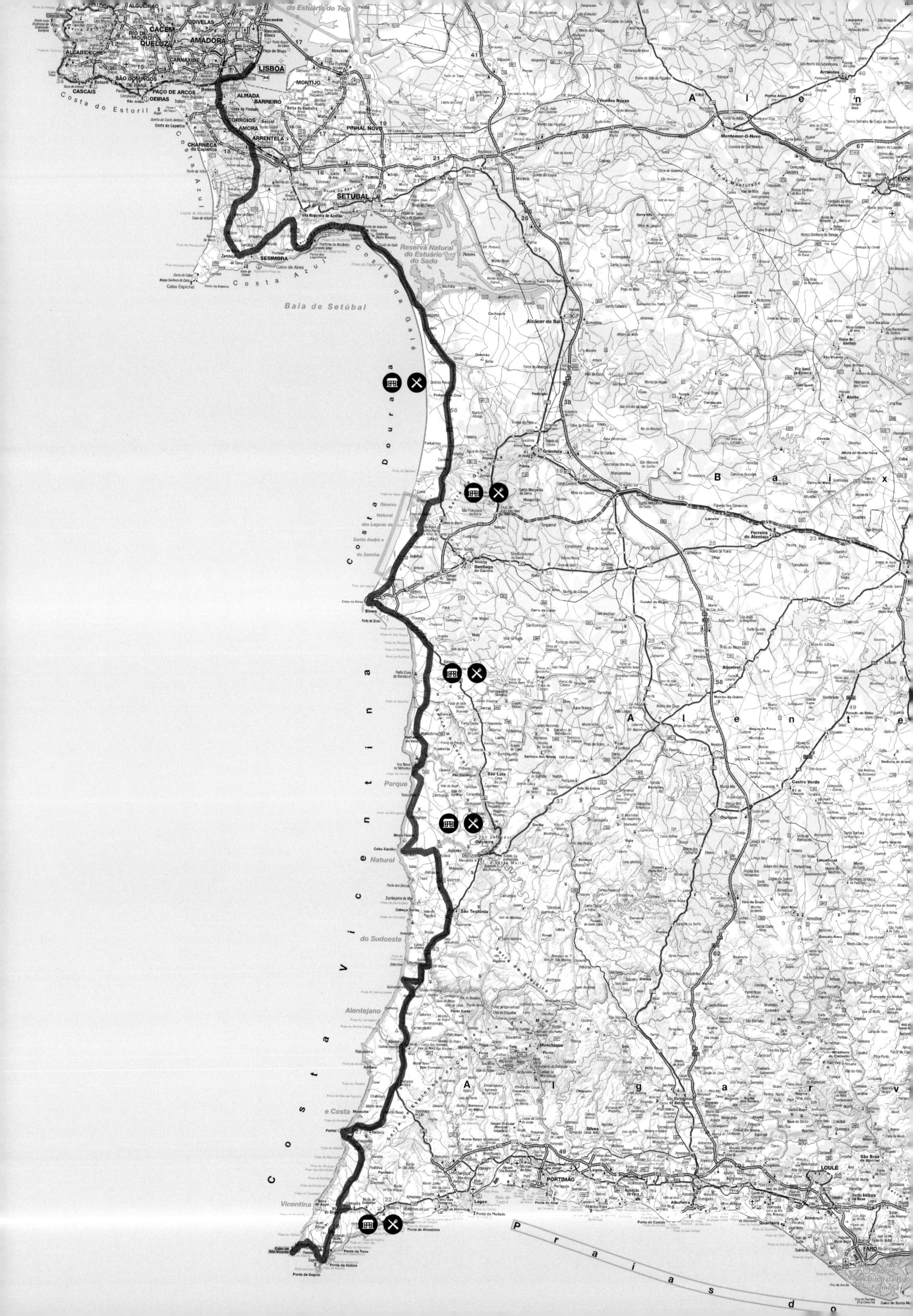
LISBOA
AMADORA
QUELUZ
CACÉM
ODIVELAS
CASCAIS
OEIRAS
ALMADA
BARREIRO
MONTIJO
SETÚBAL
SESIMBRA
PINHAL NOVO
Costa do Estoril
Costa Azul
Baía de Setúbal
Reserva Natural do Estuário do Sado
Costa da Galé
Costa Dourada
Alcácer do Sal
Grândola
Santiago do Cacém
Sines
Reserva Natural das Lagoas de Santo André e da Sancha
Montemor-O-Novo
Ferreira do Alentejo
Ajustrel
Castro Verde
Ourique
Odemira
São Teotónio
Monchique
Silves
PORTIMÃO
Lagos
Albufeira
LOULÉ
FARO
Costa Vicentina
Parque Natural do Sudoeste Alentejano e Costa Vicentina
Alentejo
Baixo
Algarve
Praias do

PONTA DA PIEDADE

SAGRES TAVIRA

311 KM • 5 HOURS // 194 MILES • 5 HOURS

Beinahe transparentes Sonnenlicht schimmert über dem Atlantik und seiner sanft wogenden Wasseroberfläche. Kaum zu glauben, welche Energien hier noch vor wenigen Stunden getobt haben, von den gischtenden Wogen der Nacht ist jetzt nur noch eine Ahnung von Salz in der Luft zu spüren.

—

Almost transparent sunlight gleams over the gently rolling Atlantic. It's hard to believe the energies that were raging here just a few hours ago, there is now only a hint of salt in the air after the churning waves of the night.

PONTA DA PIEDADE

RESTAURANT

BOVINO STEAKHOUSE
QUINTA DO LAGO, ROUNDABOUT 6, RUA FORMOSA, QUINTA DO LAGO
8135-162 ALMANCIL
WWW.QUINTADOLAGO.COM/PT/RESTAURANTES/BOVINO-STEAKHOUSE/

BUTCHERS ALMANCIL
R. DO COMÉRCIO 286
8135-127 ALMANCIL

Sanfter Wind streicht uns durch das Gesicht, eine milde Morgensonne übergießt die karge Vegetation auf den Felsen am Ende Europas mit goldenem Schimmer. Tief unter uns, am Fuß der ockerfarbenen Klippen, murmelt das Meer, schwappt türkisgrüne Brandung gegen Felsblöcke, in Höhlen und Kavernen. Heute beginnt unsere letzte Etappe, beinahe etwas wehmütig geben wir uns den Erinnerungen an die vielen Kilometer dieser Reise hin: Der Start in Porto, das Toben über die Berge des Nordens und die Windungen im Tal des Douro. Portwein und trockene Hitze im Landesinneren, dann der erste Moment des Wiedersehens mit dem Atlantik. Atemberaubende Schönheit und wilde Brutalität der Wellen oben in Nazaré, dann die magische Irrfahrt durch den grünen Garten Eden des Sintra-Cascais-Naturpark. Die Ankunft in Lissabon, der Zauber dieser lichten Stadt am Ende der Welt, und schließlich – nach dem Ritt über die Serra da Arrábida und der Fährfahrt zur Halbinsel Troia – der lange Weg nach Süden. 1000 Bilder laufen vor unserem inneren Auge ab und heute werden wir auf dieser letzten Etappe noch einmal besonders bunte hinzufügen.

Jetzt aber erst einmal: Rock 'n' Roll. Raus aus Sagres, dann der Sprint über das flache Plateau des Kaps bis hinauf nach Vola do Bispo und dort nach Osten. Zuerst am Fuß der Berge entlang, dann für den schnellen Koffein-Schuss eines „Bica" oder auf einen sanften „Galao" nach Burgau, ans Meer. Und schon kann es weitergehen, nach Lagos. Dort nehmen wir Anlauf, stürmen nach Norden und branden gegen die Berge. Schwingen dann in die ersten Hügel hinein, während wir von jungen Pinien verfolgt werden, die als ganze Schulen in Reih und Glied stramm stehen, um einmal wieder Wald zu werden. Vorbei am Stausee der Barragem da bravura und dann immer weiter, durch ein Land, das beinahe schon an Südostasien erinnert. Mit seinen dramatischen Hügeln, den verzauberten Winkeln und der nun ins Land ziehenden Tageshitze. Bei Marmelete haben wir die Serra de Monchique erreicht und werfen nun eine Münze: den Gebirgszug im Norden auf unzähligen Kurven umrunden und auf der N266 weiter bis ans Ende des Bezirks Faro fahren, oder südlich bleiben, Dörfer und

A gentle breeze brushes our faces, a mild morning sun pours its golden rays over the sparse vegetation on the rocks at the end of Europe. Far below us, at the foot of the ochre-colored cliffs, the sea swishes, turquoise-green waves wash on the rocks, into caves and caverns. Today our final leg begins, with a touch of melancholy we surrender to the memories of the many kilometers of this journey: The start in Porto, the romp over the mountains in the north and the twists and turns through the Douro Valley. Port wine and dry heat inland, then the first moment of being reunited with the Atlantic. The breathtaking beauty and wild brutality of the waves up at Nazaré, followed by the magical odyssey through the green Garden of Eden in the Sintra-Cascais Nature Park. Our arrival in Lisbon, the magic of this light city at the end of the continent, and finally – after a ride over the Serra da Arrábida and the ferry trip to the Troia Peninsula – the long stretch south. A thousand images run through our minds and today, on this last stage, we'll add a particularly colorful memory.

But first let's enjoy a bit of Rock 'n' Roll. We leave Sagres, sprint over the flat plains of the cape and up to Vola do Bispo before veering east. First tracing the foot of the mountains, then for a quick caffeine shot of "Bica" or the more merciful "Galao" to Burgau, to the ocean. On to Lagos. There, we take a run-up, storm north and crash against the mountains. We swing into the first foothills, pursued by sapling pines standing at attention in rank and file, waiting to grow and become a forest again. Past the reservoir at Barragem da bravura and onwards, ever onwards, through a country that looks almost Southeast Asian. With its dramatic hills, enchanted corners and the daytime heat now seeping inland. At Marmelete, we've reached the Serra de Monchique, and now flip a coin: should we take the northern cordillera loop with countless curves and the N266 in the direction of the Faro district or continue south, exploring villages and farmland. The coin has barely hit the ground and we're on our way – north, of course. The road snakes through the mountains like a rollercoaster gone wild and suddenly a function that normally stays on standby

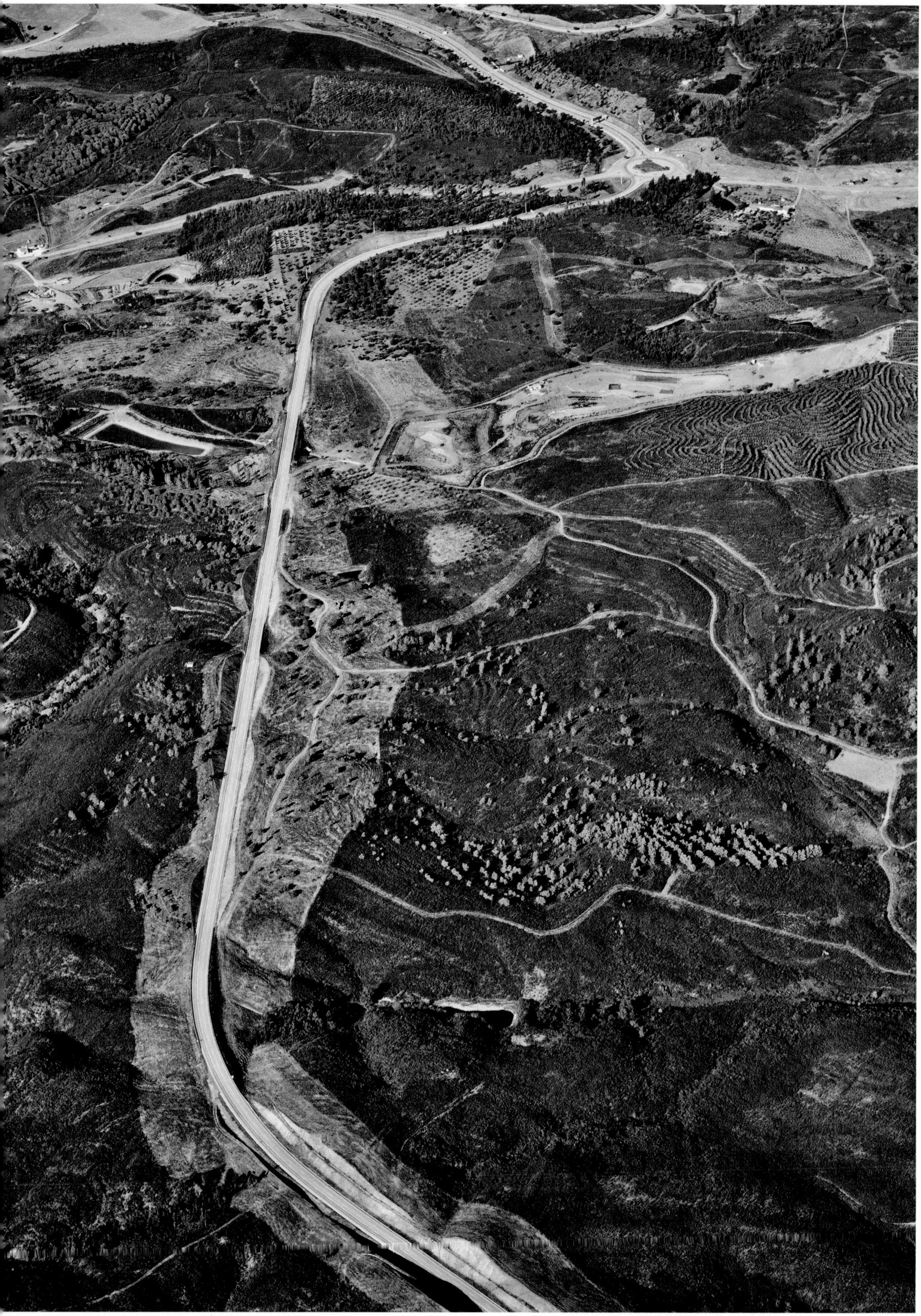

LAGO'S

AUTÓDROMO
INTERNACIONAL DO
ALGARVE

PARQUE DA BARRAGEM
DE ODELOUCA

PARQUE DA BARRAGEM DE ODELOUCA

N397

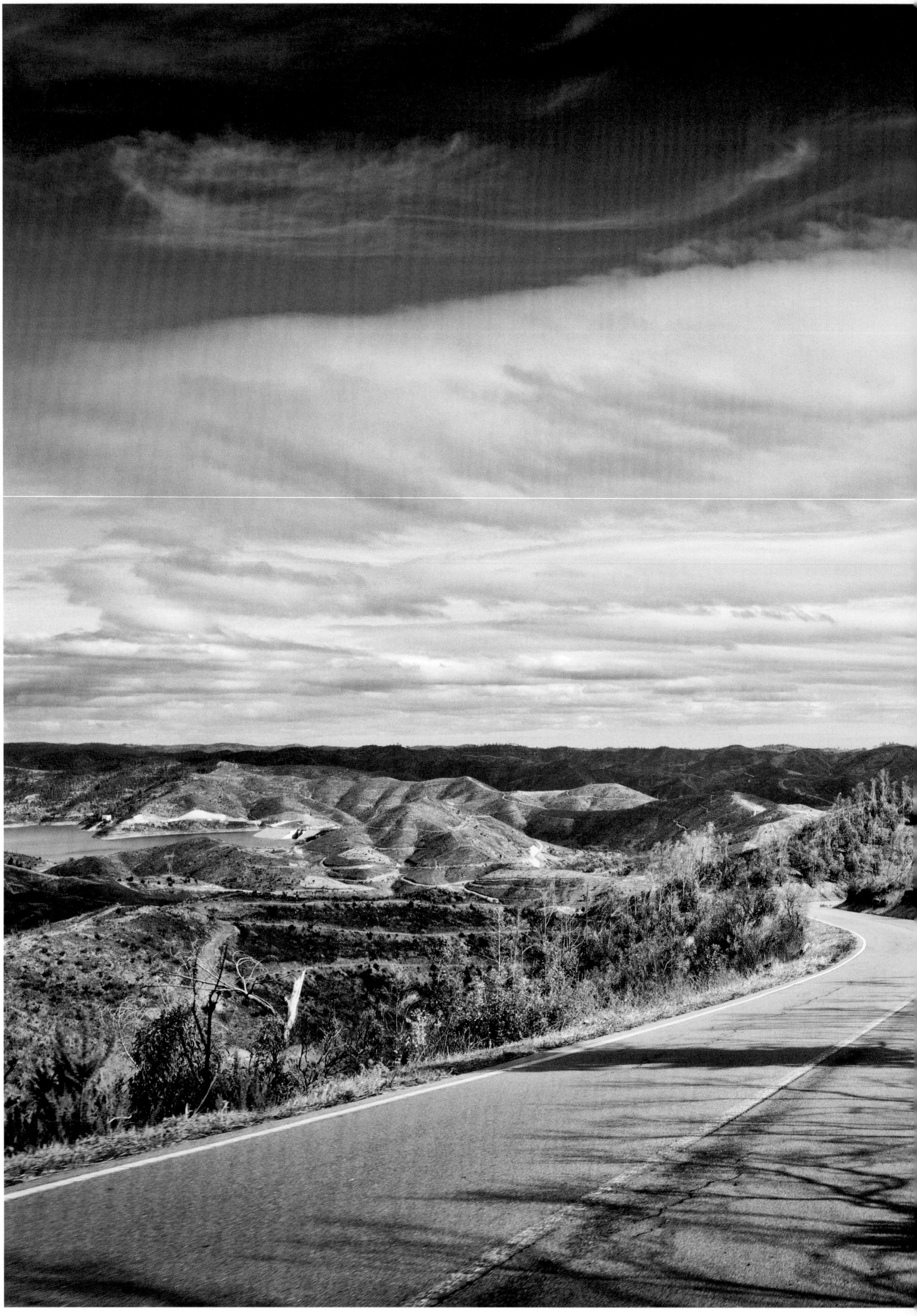

RESTAURANT

MARISQUEIRA RUI
R. COMENDADOR VILARINHO 27
8300-148 SILVES
WWW.MARISQUEIRARUI.PT

RESTAURANTE O TEODÓSIO
R. DO EMIGRANTE 50
8200-440 ALBUFEIRA
WWW.TEODOSIOREIDOSFRANGOS.PT

A TIA BIA
N2/N 124
WWW.ATIABIA.COM

Kulturland durchstreifen. Die Münze hat kaum den Boden berührt, da sind wir bereits unterwegs – nach Norden natürlich. Wie eine wildgewordene Achterbahn kurvt die Straße durch die Berge und plötzlich springt bei uns eine Funktion an, die sonst immer auf Standby mitläuft: die Rangliste der durchgedrehtesten Kurvenstrecken des Planeten. Wir hüten diese Liste wie eine Kostbarkeit, man muss es als Straße wirklich in sich haben, um eine Chance auf Erwähnung zu sehen, die Liste führt Klassiker und Unerwartetes, große Namen und Underdogs und jetzt beginnen Codes rot zu blinken: M1067, M501, N266 – von Marmelete nach Monchique, von Selão nach Nave Redonda. Mit jeder Kurve rutscht diese Strecke in unserer Hitliste weiter nach vorne und landet auf den epischen Plätzen der Geheimtipps. Prädikat: unbedingt hinfahren, wenn man in der Ecke ist. – Korkeichen und Eukalyptus stehen als euphorisierte Zuschauer am Straßenrand, während wir uns in Trance fahren. Die Kurven haben einen geschmeidigen Rhythmus, selbst die Geraden winden sich mit sanftem Hüftschwung, keine ist länger als ein halb ausgedrehter Gang. Immer wieder tun sich Ausblicke in die Hügel auf, dann wird das Asphaltband von roten Felswänden und dichter Vegetation verschluckt. Sagenhaft.

Hinter Nave Redonda könnten wir einfach in die trockenen Hügel des Landesinneren hineinfahren, aber wir drehen um. Wir haben eine Verabredung unten im Süden. Rocken zurück, über Monchique und Casais in Richtung Portimão, beinahe bis Vidigal, und dort biegen wir nach rechts ab: Autódromo Internacional do Algarve steht auf dem Straßenschild. Racing ahead. Wir haben es sogar geschafft, uns auf die Strecke zu mogeln, für eine Runde Vollgas. Und deshalb: Feuer frei! Die lange Start- und Zielgerade hinunter, mit kurz stockendem Herzschlag in die entsetzlich schnelle Doppelrechtskurve am Ende, noch einmal nach rechts Luftholen und dann vollkommen blind über eine Kuppe-plus-Linkskurve. Jetzt bist du adäquat eingeschüchtert und hellwach, vollgepumpt mit Adrenalin und bereit für die nächste Ecke: einen trockenen Bergauf-Linksknick, der ganz harmlos am Ende einer nach unten abfallenden Geraden auf dich wartet. Spitz übers Eck – und jetzt

comes on: the ranking list of the craziest twisty roads on the planet. We guard this list like a treasure, a road really has to be extraordinary to warrant a mention. Topping the list are the classics, the unexpected, the big names and underdogs... but now the codes begin to blink red: M1067, M501, N266 – from Marmelete to Monchique, from Selão to Nave Redonda. With every corner, this route moves further up the hit list and lands amongst the epic places for insider tips – definitely go there if you're in the area. Cork oaks and eucalyptus stand at the side of the road like euphoric spectators as we drive ourselves into a trance. The curves take on a smooth rhythm, even the straights sashay along with a gentle hip swing, none longer than reaching half the redline of a gear. Again and again, we get glimpses of the rolling hills before red rock walls and dense vegetation swallow up the asphalt strip. Phenomenal.

After Nave Redonda we could simply drive into the arid hills of the country's interior, but we turn around. We have a rendezvous in the south. Back we roll, over Monchique and Casais towards Portimão, just before Vidigal we take a right turn at the sign for the Autódromo Internacional do Algarve. Racing ahead. We even manage to talk our way onto the track for one flying lap. And therefore: flat out from here. At the end of the long start-finish straight, with hearts in our throats, a frightening double right-hander, another gulp of air, then right and over a blind crest plus left-hander.

Now we're adequately intimidated and wide away, pumped full of adrenaline and ready for the next corner: a sudden uphill kink to the left waits harmlessly at the bottom of a downward straight. Sharp through the turn – and now you realize that the corner is already behind you, that the exit is wide and open, that you're picking wild flowers in the grass and the whole world is laughing at you, while even children could overtake you on tricycles. So, full throttle. Error correction. You think. And that's the exact moment when this corner takes you by the hand, pulls you aside and says: "Look, that's not how you do it. You don't simply correct mistakes on the racetrack, either

N397

„Auf Rennstrecken korrigiert man Fehler nicht einfach. Du machst es von Anfang an richtig oder du lässt es bleiben. Dummy." – Zurück für einen zweiten Versuch darfst du nach dieser freundlichen Ermahnung trotzdem nicht.

stellst du fest, dass die Kurve bereits zu Ende ist, dass der Ausgang breit und weit ist, dass du blümchenpflückend in der Gegend stehst und die ganze Welt über dich lacht, während gleich Kinder auf Dreirädern an dir vorbeiziehen werden. Deshalb: Vollgas. Fehlerkorrektur. Denkst du. Und genau das ist der Moment, in dem diese Ecke dich an die Hand nimmt, zur Seite führt und sagt: „Schau mal, so kannst du das nicht machen. Auf Rennstrecken korrigiert man Fehler nicht einfach. Du machst es von Anfang an richtig oder du lässt es bleiben. Dummy." – Zurück für einen zweiten Versuch darfst du nach dieser freundlichen Ermahnung trotzdem nicht. Du gehst wild entschlossen ans Gas, stehst ein Augenzwinkern später gewaltig quer, hast alle Hände voll zu tun, trotz flugzeugträgerbreiter Strecke nicht doch noch ins Aus zu segeln, und rollst dann mit hochrotem Kopf weiter. Peinlich.

Nochmal blind links, dann markant rechts ... und an der mächtigen Gegengeraden-Senke hinter der Start-Ziel-Tribüne beißt du das erste Mal ins Lenkrad. Spürst, wie dir am tiefsten Punkt etwas schummrig wird, surfst grinsend weiter, beginnst diese wunderbare Berg-und-Talbahn tatsächlich zu mögen. – Am Eingang der Boxengasse winkt jemand: Eine Runde war abgemacht, du sollst raus. Aber das geht jetzt nicht. In der nächsten Runde wirst du zeigen, wo der Hammer hängt. Oder eben in der darauf. Oder spätestens ...

Hinter Silves, unten am Meer in Galé legen wir später einen Zwischenstopp ein und fremdschämen uns für den Gasfuß-Spirit, der so plötzlich die komplette Voodoo-Kontrolle an sich gerissen hat. Zuerst die Pastel de Natas-Fressattacke in Lissabon, jetzt der Moment, als wir nur per Safety Car-Einsatz von der Strecke abgedrängt werden konn

"You don't simply correct mistakes on the race-track, either do it right or not at all. Dummy." You can't go back for a second attempt after this friendly admonition.

do it right or not at all. Dummy." You can't go back for a second attempt after this friendly admonition. You put your foot down and a blink later you're busy trying not to sail into the greens, despite the stretch as wide as an aircraft carrier, then roll on red-faced. Embarrassing.

Another blind left, then a sharp right – and you grip the steering wheel for the first time at the mighty dip along the back straight behind the start-finish grandstand. Feel how you get a little woozy as you bottom out slightly, surfing on with a wide grin, you actually begin to enjoy this wonderful rollercoaster ride. At the pit lane entrance someone waves you in: One lap only, you need to come in. But not right now. In the next lap you'll show them how it really goes, or the one after that. Or at the latest...

After Silves, down by the ocean at Galé, we take a short break and feel a bit ashamed of the petrol-head spirit that suddenly

RESTAURANT

NÓ DE GOSTO
PRAÇA DR. ANTÓNIO PADINHA 11
8800-637 TAVIRA
WWW.NODEGOSTO.COM

ten – dieses Portugal macht etwas mit uns. Eigentlich wollten wir jetzt geradewegs am Meer entlang bis ans Ziel unserer Reise in Tavira fahren, aber in diesem Zustand vollkommener mentaler Kurven-Verwahrlosung sind wir nicht bereit für eine Rückkehr in die Zivilisation. Da hilft nur ein kontemplative Bußrunde in den Bergen. Und deshalb lassen wir das Meer noch einmal hinter uns zurück, fahren an Albufeira vorbei bis Boliqueime und dort nach Nordosten. In Castelhana geht es los, wir schlenzen nach Salhir, dann auf die Straße nach Norden. In die Hügel Portugals. Erst als wir die von Norden heranrauschende N2 treffen, fühlen wir uns geläutert genug, um den Weg nach Süden anzutreten.

Einen letzten Rückfall ins Leben des zügellos umherstreifenden CURVES-Nomaden erleiden wir kurz vor Barranco do Velho – wo doch die N124 so herrlich verlockend nach Cachopo streift –, dann vertrauen wir uns der N397 an. Klar. Moderat. Ruhig. Wie das tiefblaue Meer der Algarve an einem goldenen Sommersonnenabend.

seized total voodoo control. First the Pastel de Natas binge in Lisbon, now the moment where we could only be forced from the track by a safety car – Portugal is doing something to us. The plan was to drive along the coast to our destination in Tavira, but in this state of complete mental curve craze, we're not yet ready to return to civilization. Only a contemplative repentant tour in the mountains can help. And so, we again leave the sea behind us, drive past Albufeira to Boliqueime and from there to the northeast. It begins in Castelhana, we stroll to Salhir, then take the road north. Into the hills of Portugal. Only when we meet up with the N2 rushing in from the north do we feel chastened enough make our way south.

We suffer one last relapse in the life of the rampaging CURVES nomads shortly before Barranco do Velho – where the N124 so wonderfully lures us to Cachopo – before we entrust ourselves to the N397. Clear. Moderate. Calm. Like the deep blue sea of the Algarve on a golden summer evening.

HOTEL & RESTAURANT

COMPANHIA DAS CULTURAS
FAZENDA S. BARTOLOMEU
8950-270 CASTRO MARIM
WWW.COMPANHIADASCULTURAS.COM

SAGRES TAVIRA

Der Süden Portugals – das ist Schauplatz der letzten Etappe unserer Reise. Vom São Vicente-Kap bei Sagres bis zur Grenze nach Spanien sind wir unterwegs, fahren diese rund 150 Kilometer Luftlinie natürlich aber nicht auf dem geraden Weg, sondern nehmen uns Zeit für die atemberaubenden Berge der Algarve-Region. Die stehen im Schatten der Strände des Südens, gehören für Reiseende mit CURVES im Herzen aber zu den starken Attraktionen dieser südwestlichsten Ecke Europas. Ein weiter Bogen von Lagos ins Gebirge von Monchique bis wieder hinunter nach Portimão führt uns in entlegene Regionen, auf schmale und verwunschene Straßen, in eine Welt mit gemächlichem Gang. Zurück in der Küstenregion legen wir einen Zwischenstopp ein, der vom exakten Gegenteil geprägt ist: Vollgas. – Die hügelige und vertrackt zu fahrende Rennstrecke von Portimão steht seit Jahren im Kalender der Superbike- und MotoGP-Weltmeisterschaften, 2020 ist sogar die Formel Eins hier zu Gast. Nach dieser schwungvollen Party-Einlage neigt sich unsere Fahrt durch Portugal nun tatsächlich ihrem Ende entgegen, nur noch eine letzte Runde führt uns als Absacker zurück in das stille Land, das wir so sehr ins Herz geschlossen haben – dann landen wir dort, wo alle Geschichten dieser großen Fahrt beginnen und enden: am Meer.

—

Portugal's south is the scene of the last stage of our trip. We head from Cape St. Vincent near Sagres to the Spanish border - almost 150 kilometers as the crow flies, but not in a straight line, of course. We take our time through the breathtaking mountains of the Algarve region. They lack the fame of the south's beaches, but in keeping with the CURVES spirit, they belong to the major attractions of this south-western corner of Europe. Another wide arc from Lagos into the mountains of Monchique all the way down to Portimão, narrow, magical roads lead us to remote regions, into a world with a leisurely pace. Back at the coast, we make a detour that brings the exact opposite: full throttle. The rollercoaster racetrack of Portimão has hosted Superbike and Moto Grand Prix World Championships for years, and in 2020, even Formula One pays a visit. After this lively party performance, our trip through Portugal is now coming to an end – but just one last lap leads us back to the quiet country that we've come to love. We end up there, where every story of great journeys begins and ends: at the sea.

311 KM • 5 HOURS // 194 MILES • 5 HOURS

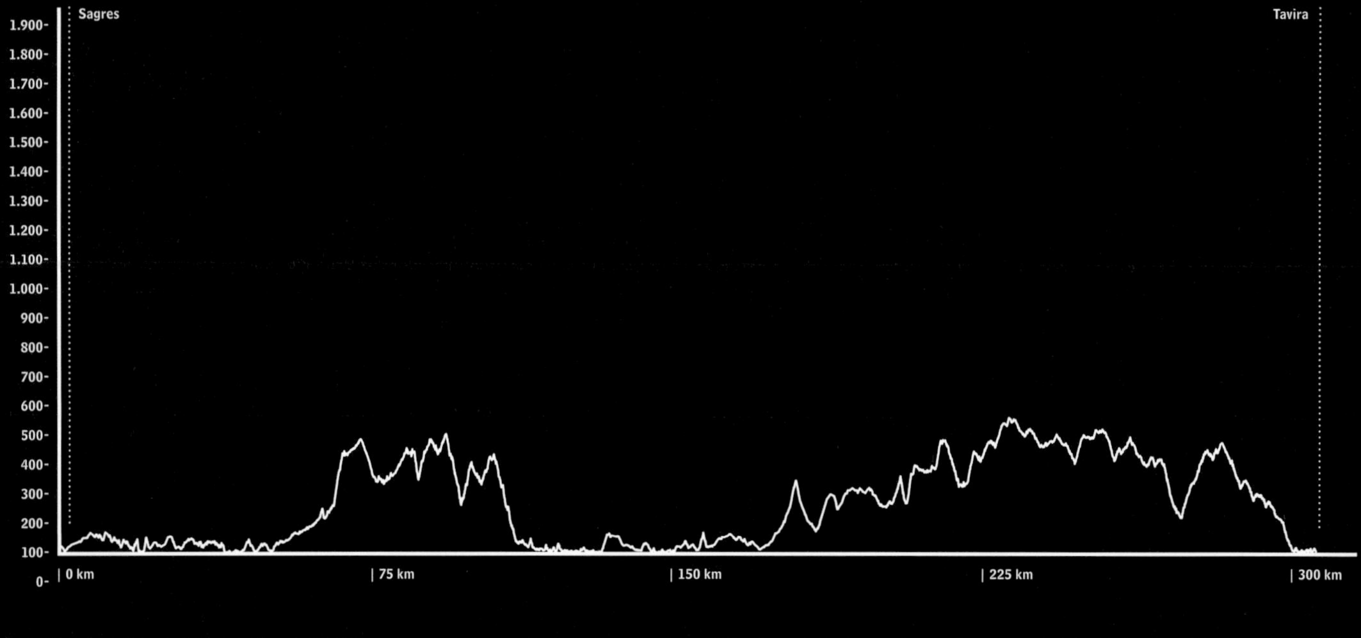

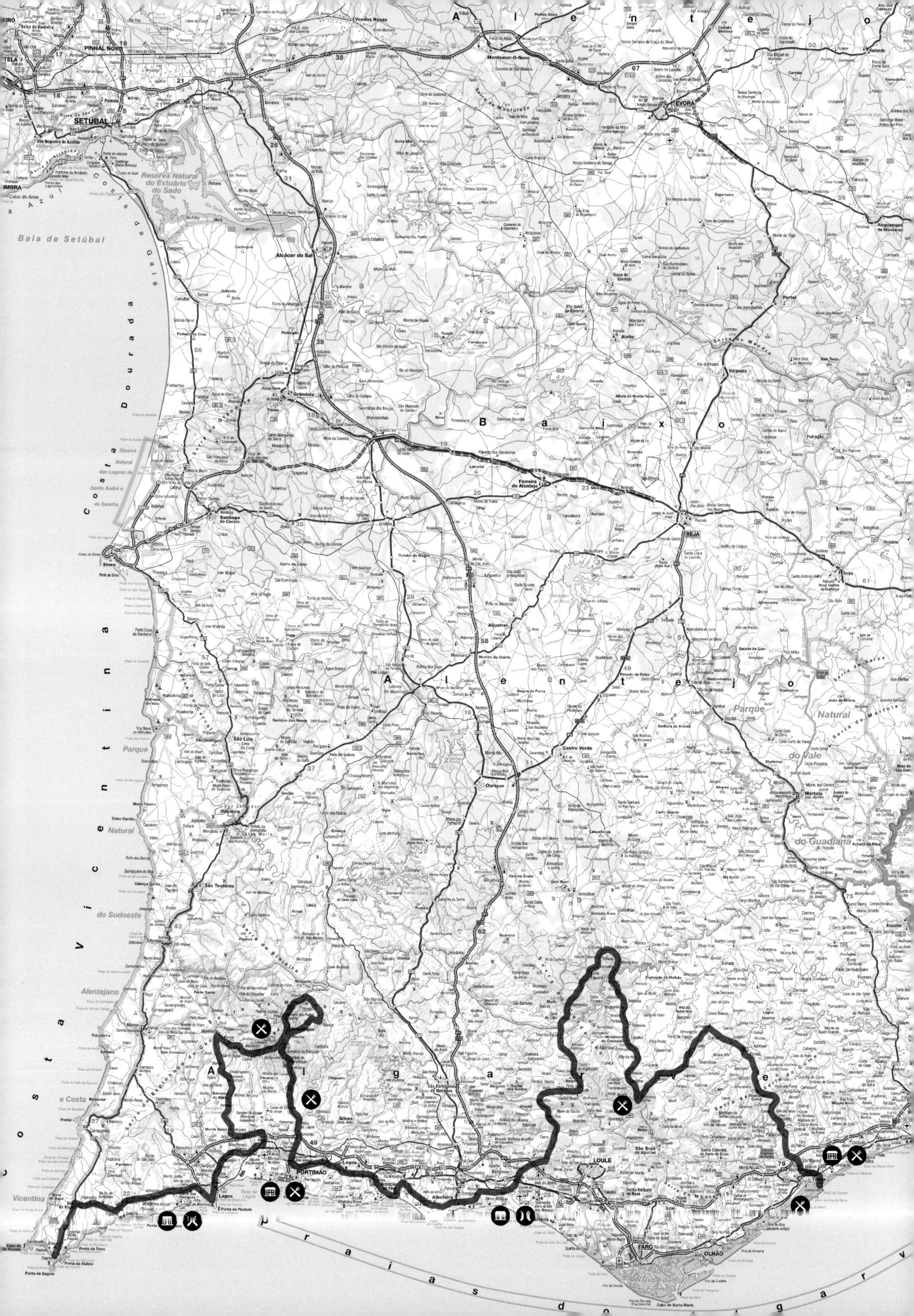

A l e n t e j o
B a i x o
A l e n t e j o
A l g a r v e
Costa Vicentina
Costa Dourada
Costa Azul
Costa da Galé
Praias do Algarve
Baia de Setúbal
Reserva Natural do Estuário do Sado
Parque Natural do Sudoeste Alentejano e Costa Vicentina
Parque Natural do Vale do Guadiana
Setúbal
Pinhal Novo
Palmela
Vendas Novas
Montemor-O-Novo
Évora
Reguengos de Monsaraz
Alcácer do Sal
Grândola
Viana do Alentejo
Alvito
Portel
Vidigueira
Cuba
Ferreira do Alentejo
Beja
Serpa
Santiago do Cacem
Sines
Aljustrel
Castro Verde
Mértola
Ourique
Odemira
São Teotónio
São Luís
Alcoutim
Portimão
Lagos
Albufeira
Silves
Loulé
São Brás de Alportel
Faro
Olhão
Tavira
Cabo de São Vicente
Sagres
Cabo de Santa Maria

DEUS EX
MACHINA

ASK A LOCAL

Ricardo ist autoverrückt im besten Sinne. Jemand mit Benzin im Blut und nicht weniger als drei Porsche in der Garage. Nebenbei ist er aber auch Gründer von Coolnvintage und macht aus alten Land Rovern fahrende Kunstwerke. Über sich selbst sagt er: „Ich bin von Natur aus neugierig und fühle ich mich in der Stille und Ruhe der freien Natur am wohlsten. Ich liebe das Verhältnis der Dinge zueinander. Eigentlich war ich aber auch immer schon ein Petrolhead, was mich dazu gebracht hat, meistens unbefestigte Straßen zu nehmen. Ich bin vor allem von Kunst und Design beeinflusst und glaube, dass Dinge handwerklich perfekt sein und ewig halten sollten. Wenn sie kaputt gehen, sollten sie repariert und nicht entsorgt werden. Wir sollten weniger kaufen und dafür das nutzen, was wir haben. Ich liebe das Essen und das Fahren, allerdings nicht zur selben Zeit."

–

Ricardo is crazy about cars in the best sense of the word. Someone with gasoline in his blood and no less than three Porsche in his garage. He is also the founder of Coolnvintage and turns old Land Rovers into moving works of art. This is what he says about himself: "Curious by nature I feel most at home in the stillness and peacefulness of the great outdoors. I love the scale of things. Being a petrolhead by lineage led me to search for the dirt road most times. I'm influenced mostly by art and design and believe things should be well built and last forever. When they break they should be fixed and not disposed of. We should buy less and use what we have more. I love to eat and drive – not at the same time."

Portugal in drei Worten? Sonne, Salz, gegrillter Fisch.

Lissabon oder Porto? Lissabon im Sommer, Porto im Winter.

Welches Lied ist Portugals ultimativer Soundtrack? Alles von der Band Dead Combo.

Welche portugiesischen Geheimtipps würdest du gern an die große Glocke hängen? Wo muss man gewesen sein? Was muss man gesehen haben?

Portugal in three words? Sun, salt, grilled fish.

Lisbon or Porto? Lisbon in the summer, Porto in winter.

Which song is Portugal's ultimate soundtrack? Everything by the band Dead Combo.

Which Portugal insider tips would you like to shout from the rooftops? Where must one have been? What do you have to see? What do you really have to do in Portugal? 1. You have to eat in someone's house or a family

Was muss man in Portugal unbedingt tun? 1. Du musst bei jemandem zu Hause oder in einem familiengeführten Restaurant essen. Nimm dir Zeit, um das Essen, die Freundlichkeit der Leute und das Gespräch zu genießen.

2. Man muss die schmalen Straßen auf dem Land fahren, die kleinen Dörfer und die alten Leute sehen, die draußen vor ihren Häusern sitzen und das Leben genießen.

3. Man muss an der Küste von Sagres nach Lissabon fahren und irgendwo unterwegs „amêijoas à bulhão pato" (ein Muschelgericht) essen. Man muss auch von Porto nach Douro und Gerês fahren.

4. Geh an den Strand.

5. Trink portugiesischen Wein, es lohnt sich. Danach kannst du Lissabon und Porto besuchen und „Pasteis de Nata" essen. – Vorsicht, das ist nur die Spitze des Eisbergs bei portugiesischen Süßigkeiten. Nur zu!

Was ist Portugals Lieblingsessen und warum? Frischer gegrillter Fisch und Meeresfrüchte. Weil es auf einfachste Weise zubereitet wird, nur mit Salz und etwas Olivenöl, und das lässt die Qualität der Zutaten in den Vordergrund treten. Ich glaube nicht, dass frische Meeresfrüchte oder gegrillter Fisch irgendwo auf der Welt besser schmecken.

Was ist portugiesische Lebensart? Das Leben wird in einem langsameren Tempo gelebt. Wir nehmen uns Zeit, das Essen, Familie und Freunde zu genießen. Auch das gute Wetter. Mahlzeiten dauern ewig (und das ist auch gut so). Das Essen schmeckt erstaunlich und der Tisch ist immer voll. Wir halten die Dinge einfach.

Welche schlechte Angewohnheit ist typisch portugiesisch? Zuspätkommen.

Wenn man es nie nach Portugal schafft, welches andere Land ist ein guter Ersatz? Italien.

Was ist die schönste Straße in Portugal? Die Serra da Estrela.

Welches Auto ist ideal für Portugal? Du brauchst zwei: einen Land Rover (möglichst von Coolnvintage restauriert, ich habe gehört, die sind erstaunlich), um die ganze Küste und all die erstaunlichen Offroad-Pisten erkunden zu können, und einen 911, nur um die Serra da Arrábida am Samstagmorgen zu fahren. Besorg dir eine „Torta de Azeitão" (ein Gebäck mit Zitrone und Zimt), während du dort bist.

owned restaurant. Take your time to enjoy the meal, the kindness of the people and the conversation.

2. You have to drive the narrow roads in the countryside, see the small villages and the old people sitting outside in front of their houses, just enjoying life.

3. You have to drive on the coast from Sagres to Lisbon and eat some "amêijoas à bulhão pato" (a clam dish) somewhere along the way. You also have to drive from Porto to Douro and Gerês.

4. You have to go to the beach.

5. Drink some Portuguese wine, it's worth it. After that you can visit Lisbon and Porto and eat some "Pasteis de Nata" – beware as these are only the tip of the iceberg regarding Portuguese sweets. Dig deeper!

What is Portugal's favorite food and why? Freshly grilled fish and seafood. Because it's prepared in the simplest way, just salt and some olive oil and that lets the quality of the ingredients take the main stage. I don't think fresh seafood or grilled fish taste better anywhere in the world.

What is the Portuguese way of life? Life is lived at a slower pace. We take our time to enjoy food, family and friends. Also the good weather. Meals take forever (and that's a good thing), the food tastes amazing and the table is always full. We keep it simple.

Which bad habit is typically Portuguese? Being late.

If you never make it to Portugal - which other country is a good replacement visit? Italy.

What is the most beautiful street in Portugal? It's a road, Serra da Estrela.

Which car is ideal for Portugal? You need two: a Land Rover (restored by Coolnvintage, if at all possible, I hear they're amazing) so you can explore all the coast and all the amazing offroad tracks, and a 911, just to do Serra da Arrábida on Saturday mornings. Get a "Torta de Azeitão" (a pastry with lemon and cinnamon) while you're there.

Instagram: Coolnvintage

37

DEUS
CUSTOMS

COOLNVINTAGE

BIG BANGER
MATCHBOX
BIG BANGER
new 26

LES 24 HEURES DU MANS
REF. 430
LES 24 HEURES DU MANS
DUNLOP
SHELL

U.S.A.

WORTH A VISIT: CARAMULO MUSEUM

CARAMULO MUSEUM
RUA JEAN LURÇAT 42
3475-031 CARAMULO
INFO@MUSEU-CARAMULO.NET
WWW.MUSEU-CARAMULO.NET

Im Jahr 1921 gründete der Arzt Jerónimo de Lacerda das Dorf Caramulo und begann dort mit dem Bau des größten Sanatoriums des Landes, ja sogar der iberischen Halbinsel. In den folgenden Jahrzehnten machte der medizinische Fortschritt diese Einrichtung zunehmend obsolet, sodass seine beiden Söhne Abel und João nach Ideen suchten, um das Überleben des Ortes und des Bauwerks zu sichern. In den 50er-Jahren eröffneten sie ein Museum und schufen damit ein ungewöhnliches Zentrum für Kunst und Kultur – hoch oben auf einem Berg und im Landesinneren gelegen. Die ungewöhnliche Sammlung besteht aus 500 Gemälden, Skulpturen, Möbeln, Keramiken und Wandteppichen, die vom alten Ägypten bis zu Picasso reichen. Ein zweites Gebäude beherbergt 100 Automobile und Motorräder aus der Sammlung von João de Lacerda. Das Museu do Caramulo ist das ganze Jahr über geöffnet und hat seit seiner Gründung mehr als eineinhalb Millionen Besucher empfangen.

In 1921, the doctor Jerónimo de Lacerda founded the village of Caramulo and began building the largest sanatorium in the country – indeed, in the Iberian Peninsula. Over the following decades, medical progress made this facility increasingly obsolete.

Hence, his two sons Abel and João started searching for ideas to ensure the survival of the town and the building. In the 1950s, they opened a museum and thus created an unusual center for art and culture – high up on a mountain in the country's interior. The extraordinary collection consists of 500 paintings, sculptures, furniture, ceramics and tapestries ranging from ancient Egypt to Picasso.

A second building is home to 100 cars and motorbikes from the João de Lacerda collection. The Museu do Caramulo is open all year round and has welcomed more than 1.5 million visitors since its opening.

TASK of the DAY
BE HAPPY

BACKSTAGE

In unserer Erinnerung ist Portugal ein farbstichiger Super-8-Film: strahlende Kinder in etwas zu großen Badehosen an einem Algarve-Strand. Nasse Haare kleben am Kopf, die Augen leuchten und die Zähne klappern, ein Handtuch wird fröstelnd um die Schultern geschlungen. Vaters Stimme gibt Regieanweisungen aus dem Off und die 40 Jahre jüngere Ausgabe unserer Mutter rettet lachend das Eis am Stiel vor einem Ende im Sand. Aber da sind auch die anderen Schnappschüsse: Klassenfahrt nach Lissabon, wilde Frisuren, zu weite Hosen, zu enge T-Shirts und ein Gefühl von Freiheit und Bedeutung – wir sind Rockstars, Helden, heiße Sonnen im Mittelpunkt eines mediterranen Universums. Und ziemlich privilegiert: Damals haben es nur wenige nach Portugal geschafft; Italien, Spanien und Frankreich kommen in den Urlaubserinnerungen unserer Altersgenossen deutlich häufiger vor. Der Weg bis ans südwestliche Ende des europäischen Kontinents ist einfach zu weit. Natürlich mussten wir zurückkommen, Portugal noch einmal sehen, alte Erinnerungen bergen. Und trotzdem dieses Land ganz neu erleben. Denn

In our memory, Portugal is a slightly faded Super 8 film: Radiant children in slightly oversized swimming costumes on a beach in the Algarve. Wet hair clinging to their heads, eyes shining and teeth chattering, a towel flung over their shoulders, shivering. Dad's voice shouts directions from offstage and our then 40-years-younger mother laughs as she saves a popsicle from landing in the sand. But there are other snapshots: A class trip to Lisbon, wild hair, trousers that are too wide, t-shirts that are too tight and a feeling of freedom and meaning – we're rock stars, heroes, hot suns at the center of a Mediterranean universe. And rather privileged. At that time, very few people made it to Portugal. Vacation memories of Italy, Spain and France are much more prevalent among our peers. The journey to the south-western end of the European continent is simply too far. Of course we had to come back, to see Portugal again, and resurrect old memories – and yet experience this country anew. Because one thing was clearly evident to us: You can't recreate precious memories and past images. So, we left the family album

BAR
OSLO
CERVEJARIA
CAIS BAR
GUINNESS
ATM
S PO 1882

Wir haben deshalb die Familienalbum-Perspektive bewahrt wie sie ist und im Jetzt alles auf Null gesetzt. Statt Beach-Life und Entspannung, Stadtbummel und Kultur-Programm, stand dieses Mal die CURVES-Agenda im Mittelpunkt. Fahren, um des Fahrens willen, die reine Schönheit der Fortbewegung, Neugierde auf das Land hinter dem Horizont und: Kurven.

So, we left the family album perspective as it is and set the odometer to zero, to the present. Instead of beach life and relaxation, city strolls and a cultural program, the focus this time was on the CURVES agenda. Driving for the sake of driving, the sheer beauty of movement, curiosity about the countryside beyond the horizon... and curves.

eines war uns klar: Man kann kostbare Momente und vergangene Bilder nicht nachstellen. Wir haben deshalb die Familienalbum-Perspektive bewahrt wie sie ist und im Jetzt alles auf Null gesetzt. Statt Beach-Life und Entspannung, Stadtbummel und Kulturprogramm stand dieses Mal die CURVES-Agenda im Mittelpunkt. Fahren, um des Fahrens willen, die reine Schönheit der Fortbewegung, Neugierde auf das Land hinter dem Horizont und: Kurven. Wir müssen die Leser dieser CURVES-Ausgabe also warnen: Es wird weder um sommersonnige Erinnerungen gehen, noch um ein Bildungsprogramm. Sondern um eine vollständig neue Perspektive auf Portugal – die von der Straße. Wie immer stand nicht das Ankommen im Vordergrund, sondern das Unterwegssein. Wir haben uns deshalb bis in die letzten Winkel getraut und dabei erneut die Erfahrung gemacht, dass man nur so ein Land komplett neu entdecken und die vielen weißen Flächen auf der Landkarte bunt und lebendig machen kann.

Schon nach wenigen Kilometern hat uns dabei eine ganz bestimmte Sache in ihren Bann gezogen und nicht wieder losgelassen: Portugal lebt ein versammelt groovendes Tempo, das positive Schwingungen verbreitet. Selbst die dynamischen und umtriebigen Großstädte Lissabon und Porto verströmen eine Gelassenheit, der man sich nicht entziehen kann. Man hängt sich nicht an Effizienz-Diskussionen auf, sondern hält das Leben im Blick – gemeinhin also genau andersherum, als man es uns sonst als echtes Erfolgsrezept verkaufen möchte. Selten haben wir auf unseren Fahrten so offene und freundliche Menschen getroffen, deren Selbstbewusstsein vollkommen frei von Selbstüberschätzung und Hybris ist, gleichzeitig aber in echtes Interesse an uns Reisenden mündet. Beinahe sogar Freude. Und dann wäre da noch eine erfreulich Glanzlack-freie Bodenständigkeit, die entwaffnend ist, ansteckend und ehrlich. Wo man diese Seele ganz unverblümt erleben kann? – In den Restaurants natürlich. Portugiesisches Essen ist nie so raffiniert und distinguiert wie in Frankreich, oder so mitreißend und gefühlsstark wie in

perspective as it is and set the odometer to zero, to the present. Instead of beach life and relaxation, city strolls and a cultural program, the focus this time was on the CURVES agenda. Driving for the sake of driving, the sheer beauty of movement, curiosity about the countryside beyond the horizon... and curves. So, readers of this CURVES issue, be warned: This is not about memories of summer days or an educational tour. It's about a completely new way of seeing Portugal – a perspective from the road. As always, the focus is not on the destination, but the journey. That's why we dared to peek into the most remote corners and again realize that this is the only way to really rediscover a country and to fill the many blank areas on the map with color and life.

After just a few kilometers, something very distinctive caught us in its spell and didn't let go: Portugal lives a collective, groovy pace that spreads a positive vibe. Even the dynamic, busy cities of Lisbon and Porto exude a serenity that is impossible to resist. One doesn't get caught up with debates about efficiency, but focuses on life – the opposite of what is normally sold to us as the real recipe for success. Rarely have we encountered such open and friendly folk on our trips, people whose self-assurance is completely free of cockiness and hubris, and at the same time have a genuine interest in us travelers. Almost even joy. And then there is a refreshingly down-to-earth attitude without any glossy coating that is disarming, contagious and honest.

Where can you experience this unveiled soul? In the restaurants, of course. Portuguese food is not as refined and distinguished as in France, or as captivating and emotional as in Italy, but it is truly authentic. Wonderful. Real. You will rarely experience sophisticated menu sequences or palate fireworks, but the cooking is strong and clear. Sweet. Salty. Oily. Bitter. Tart. The ingredients are the stars on stage, and the production relies on strong individual culinary actors instead of complex arrangements:

S PO 1882

Man wird selten effektvolle Menüfolgen erleben oder Gaumen-Feuerwerke, aber es wird stark und klar gekocht. Süß. Salzig. Fettig. Bitter. Sauer.

Italien, aber es ist authentisch. Erfreulich. Echt. Man wird selten effektvolle Menüfolgen erleben oder Gaumen-Feuerwerke, aber es wird stark und klar gekocht. Süß. Salzig. Fettig. Bitter. Sauer. Und man überlässt den Zutaten die Bühne, setzt auf starke kulinarische Einzelakteure, statt auf komplexe Inszenierungen: Fisch und Meeresfrüchte, Ziege und Lamm, Rind und Innereien, Kartoffeln und Bohnen, Gemüse und das alles zusammen, als Eintopf oder Suppe. Serviert wird ohne Netz und doppelten Boden, vollkommen effektfrei. Interessanterweise gilt das sogar für die jungen Köche der modernen, urbanen Küche, die zwar Aromen aus der weiten Welt auf portugiesische Teller bringen und mit einem international orientierten Gefühl für Portionen, Ambiente und Emotion anrichten, aber nie ins Künstliche abdriften oder den Bezug zur Region verraten.

Ähnliches gilt für die Kultur Portugals, die tief und stark gelebt wird, aber trotz ihrer ungeheuren emotionalen Bandbreite bisher allen Kommerzialisierungsversuchen widersteht. Selbstverständlich platzen die Fado-Bars aus allen Nähten, die Touristen stehen bis auf die Straße hinaus – wenn dann aber der Gesang schwer und bittersüß wie Portwein im Raum steht, ahnt jeder, dass das eine Schippe zu hart und echt ist, um in leicht verdauliche Portionen als gefühlsduseliges Mitbringsel eingeschweißt zu werden. Um nur ein besonders bekanntes Element zu nennen.

An diesem Punkt ist es besonders leicht, zu einem ganz besonderen Reisegefährten zu wechseln, der uns während der drei Wochen begleitet hat: dem Porsche 911 Turbo S Cabrio, das wir von Porsche als Soulsurfer, Reisekumpel und Arbeitstier zur Verfügung gestellt bekommen haben. Es ist uns immer noch beinahe unerklärlich, wie Ingenieure es schaffen, derartige Perfektion so gefühlsecht und ungekünstelt zu arrangieren. Wie überragende Trittsicherheit mit rasiermesserscharfem Handling zusammenfindet, wie bizarre, ultimativ gewalttätige und blutig rohe Kraftentfaltung so sanft entfaltbar wird, wie mathematisches Feedback und ungerührte Kontrolle zu den besten Freunden ausgelassener Fahrfreude werden können. Die reine Emotion, Soulful Driving at its best. Einen kurzen Moment lang haben wir ja vermutet, dass es an der Cabrio-Darreichung lag, denn Portugal, das ist voller Wärme und Duft und Weltschmerz als olfaktorischer Background-Soundtrack. Du fährst durch die Berge und durch

You will rarely experience sophisticated menu sequences or palate fireworks, but the cooking is strong and clear. Sweet. Salty. Oily. Bitter. Tart.

fish and seafood, goat and lamb, beef and organ meats, potatoes and beans, vegetables and everything together as a stew or soup. Served without a safety net or double bottom, completely free of effects. Interestingly, this also applies to the young chefs of the modern, urban kitchens, who bring flavors from the big, wide world to the Portuguese plates and serve them with an internationally inspired feeling for portions, ambience and emotion, but never veer into the artificial or deny the origin in the region.

The same goes for Portugal's culture, which is deep and strong but has so far resisted all attempts at commercialization, despite its huge emotional range. Of course, the Fado bars are bursting at the seams, tourists spill out onto the streets – and when the singing is as heavy and bittersweet as port wine, everyone understands that this is a bit too much and too real to be shrink-wrapped into easily digested portions as a soppy sentimental souvenir. To name just one particularly well-known element.

At this point, it is particularly easy to switch to a very special travel companion, one that accompanied us on our three-week journey: The Porsche 911 Turbo S Cabrio lent to us from Porsche as a soul surfer, travel buddy and workhorse. It is still almost inexplicable to us how engineers manage to create such perfection in such a sensual and authentic manner. How the outstanding surefootedness is combined with razor-sharp handling, how the bizarre, ultimately violent and raw unfolding of power can be developed so gently, how mathematical feedback and unaffected control can become the best friend of wild driving pleasure. The pure emotion, soulful driving at

CARREIRA Nº 28
Chiado
Bairro Alto
C. Sodré
S. Paulo
RUA SERRA PINTO
DESFRUTA DO SABOR ORIGINAL SEM AÇÚCAR
PORSCHE
S PO 1882

Einen kurzen Moment lang haben wir ja vermutet, dass es an der Cabrio-Darreichung lag, denn Portugal, das ist voller Wärme und Duft und Weltschmerz als olfaktorischer Background-Soundtrack. Du fährst durch die Berge und durch den Duft von Wäldern, Erde und Kräutern. Du fährst am Meer entlang und fährst durch das Aroma von Weite und Tiefe, Tang und Salz.

For a brief moment, we suspected that it was the open-top because Portugal is full of warmth and fragrance and Weltschmerz delivering the heady background soundtrack. You drive through the mountains, through the fragrance of forests, earth and herbs. You drive along the ocean and through the aroma of breadth and depth, seaweed and salt.

den Duft von Wäldern, Erde und Kräutern. Du fährst am Meer entlang und fährst durch das Aroma von Weite und Tiefe, Tang und Salz. Du fährst durch die Dörfer und Städte und fährst mit der herben Begleitung von Diesel-Parfüm, überrascht von gegrilltem Hähnchen. – Aber dann haben wir diese These wieder verworfen. Der Turbo ist auch in Coupé-Form eine Granate. Ein ganz Großer. Wir haben daher beschlossen nicht mehr zu grübeln. Sondern einfach nur zu genießen. Und deshalb: Danke, Porsche, für die reine Wahrheit. Wir verstehen sie nicht, aber die Botschaft ist angekommen.

Übrigens auch bei den Portugiesen, die uns überall mit emporgereckten Daumen und anerkennendem Nicken begrüßt und verabschiedet haben, wo passiert einem das denn sonst noch: 650 PS und drumherum nur neidlose Freude. Eigentlich hätte auf den vielen hundert Kilometern in Portugal nur einer Grund zum Neid gehabt, und zwar der Fahrer unseres Lastenmuli namens Porsche Cayenne E-Hybrid. Aber auch der schien mit dem Anblick des 911 Turbo S Cabrio von hinten mehr als zufrieden, und schwärmte ansonsten von der geschmeidigen Autorität des elektrifizierten Cayenne, vom geräuschlosen Surfen, von Komfort und Kurven-Sinn.

Am Ende haben wir dann neben den Zuhausegebliebenen, den Familien und Freunden und Unterstützern und Lesern eine weitere Adresse, bei der wir uns gerne bedanken würden: dem Museo do Caramulo. Wir sind froh, euch da oben, eine Stunde von Porto entfernt, gefunden zu haben und setzen euch hiermit auf unsere Liste der bemerkenswertesten Auto-(und-so-)Museen der Welt. Immer einen Besuch wert. Wie Portugal.

its best. For a brief moment, we suspected that it was the open-top because Portugal is full of warmth and fragrance and Weltschmerz delivering the heady background soundtrack. You drive through the mountains, through the fragrance of forests, earth and herbs. You drive along the ocean and through the aroma of breadth and depth, seaweed and salt. You drive through villages and cities with the harsh accompaniment of diesel perfume, surprised by grilled chicken. But then, we disregard this idea. The Turbo is a grenade as a coupé, too. A real big caliber. Therefore, we decide to cease our pondering and instead, simply enjoy. So, thank you Porsche, for the naked truth. We don't understand it, but we got the message.

And so did the Portuguese. Wherever we went, they greeted us with a thumbs up, appreciative nods and farewells ... where else does this happen to you nowadays: 650 hp and magnanimous joy all around you. Over the hundreds of kilometers through Portugal, only one person would have had reason to envy us, and that was the driver of our Sherpa called Porsche Cayenne E-Hybrid. But he, too, seemed more than happy with the sight of the 911 Turbo S Cabriolet from behind and raved about the smooth authority of the electric Cayenne, the silent surfing, comfort and cornering prowess.

Ultimately, in addition to those who stayed at home, to our families, friends, supporters and readers, we would like to thank the Museo do Caramulo. We're delighted to have discovered you way up there, an hour out of Porto, and put you on our list as one of the world's most remarkable automobile (among other things) museums. Always worth a visit – just like Portugal.

S PO 1882

ALCOA

PARADISE

Beach
Beer

J&B
Grant's
FAMOUS GROUSE
Red Label
Four Roses
JACK DANIEL'S
Canadian Club
BUSHMILLS
DIFFICULT ROADS OFTEN LEAD TO BEAUTIFUL DESTINATIONS

S PO 1882

PORTUGAL
LISBOA

GNR

WORTH A VISIT ONE OF THE MOST BEAUTIFUL CHURCHES

IGREJA DE SÃO LOURENÇO DE ALMANCIL
R. DA IGREJA S/N
8135-027 ALMANCIL

STEERSMAN
ROASTED CODFISH, POTATO AND TURNIP GREENS
GRILLED OCTOPUS WITH
SMOKED CARROT AND PAPRIKA
18,00€
18,00€
19,50€
25,00€
SUSHI BAR
8,50€
8,50€
11,00€
SUSHI & SASHIMI

CARREIRA Nº 28
567
DESFRUTA
DO SABOR
ORIGINAL
SEM AÇÚCAR
Coca-Cola

PORSCHE
S PO 1882

FILETES ATUM EM AZEITE 2,60
MINERVA
FILETES DE CAVALA 3,30€
SARDINHAS SI PELE SI ESPINHA 3,50€
SARDINHAS "MINERVA" 2,60€
MINERVA
FILETES DE SALMÃO COM ALHO EM AZEITE

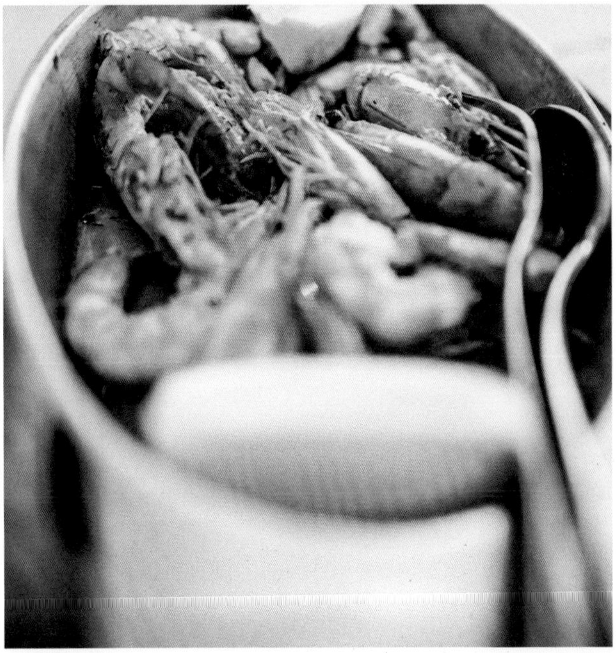

S PO 1882

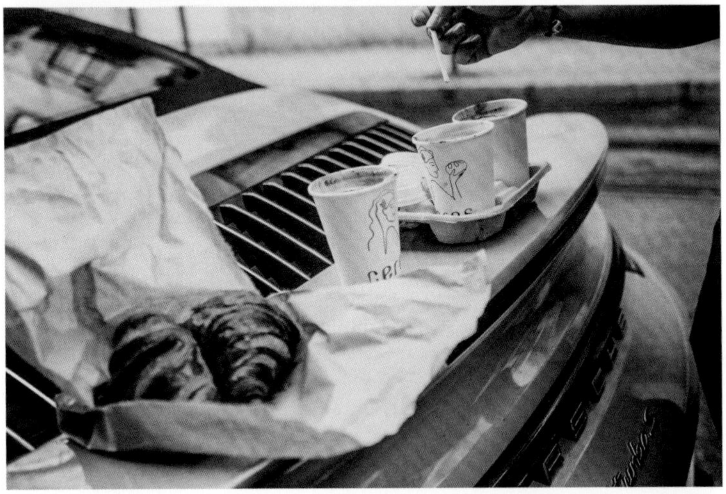

PORSCHE
S PO 1882

SARDINHAS
Luca

PENICHE

PORSCHE
S PO 1882

DANK AN / THANKS TO
BASTIAN SCHRAMM, MAXIMILIAN RAMISCH, BEN WINTER, PHILIPP HEITSCH, NADJA KNEISSLER, JÖRN HEESE, AXEL GERBER, HANNO VIENKEN, MICHAEL DORN, MICHAEL DAIMINGER, MICHAELA BOGNER

SPECIAL FX / SPECIAL FX
JOAO PEDRO • RICARDO PESSOA • NUNO & BRUNO FROM LISBON CROOKS AND SURFERS • NUNO LOBO • AIR EMOTIONS ALGARVE • PAULO FROM SEACRET BOAT TOURS
ANA RODRIGUES & PAULO PINHEIRO FROM THE PORTIMAO RACETRACK • PORSCHE LISSABON • PORSCHE PORTO FOR THEIR SUPPORT

911 Turbo S Cabriolet
Kraftstoffverbrauch/ Emissionen des Porsche 911 Turbo S Cabriolet/ Fuel consumption Porsche 911 Turbo S Cabriolet
Kraftstoffverbrauch kombiniert: 11,3 l/100 km, CO_2-Emissionen kombiniert: 257 g/km
Combined fuel consumption in accordance with EU 6: 911 Turbo S Cabriolet: 11,3 l/100 km, CO_2 emissions: 257 g/km

Cayenne E-Hybrid
Kraftstoffverbrauch/ Emissionen des Porsche Cayenne E-Hybrid/ Fuel consumption Porsche Cayenne E-Hybrid
Kraftstoffverbrauch kombiniert: 2,5-2,4 l/100 km, CO_2-Emissionen kombiniert: 58-56 g/km, Stromverbrauch kombiniert: 22,0-21,6 kWh/100 km
Combined fuel consumption in accordance with EU 6: Cayenne E-Hybrid: 2,5-2,4 l/100 km, CO_2 emissions: 58-56 g/km, Combined power consumption: 22,0-21,6 kWh/100 km

IMPRESSUM / IMPRINT

HERAUSGEBER/
PUBLISHER: CURVES MAGAZIN
THIERSCHSTRASSE 25
D-80538 MÜNCHEN

VERANTWORTLICH FÜR
DEN HERAUSGEBER/
RESPONSIBLE FOR
PUBLICATION:
STEFAN BOGNER

KONZEPT/CONCEPT:
STEFAN BOGNER
THIERSCHSTRASSE 25
D-80538 MÜNCHEN
SB@CURVES-MAGAZIN.COM

DELIUS KLASING
CORPORATE PUBLISHING
SIEKERWALL 21
D-33602 BIELEFELD

REDAKTION/
EDITORIAL CONTENT:
STEFAN BOGNER
BEN WINTER

ART DIRECTION, LAYOUT,
FOTOS/ART DIRECTION,
LAYOUT, PHOTOS:
STEFAN BOGNER

MAKING OF FOTOS:
MICHAEL DAIMINGER
PHILIPP HEITSCH

TEXT/TEXT: BEN WINTER
TEXT INTRO/TEXT INTRO:
BEN WINTER

MOTIVAUSARBEITUNG
LITHOGRAPHIE/SATZ/

POST-PRODUCTION,
LITHOGRAPHY/SETTING:
MICHAEL DORN

KARTENMATERIAL/MAP
MATERIAL: MAIRDUMONT,
OSTFILDERN

ÜBERSETZUNG/TRANSLATION
KAYE MUELLER

PRODUKTIONSLEITUNG/
PRODUCTION MANAGEMENT:
AXEL GERBER/JÖRN HEESE

DRUCK/PRINT:
KUNST- UND WERBEDRUCK
BAD OEYNHAUSEN

1.AUFLAGE/1ST EDITION:
ISBN 978-3-667-12078-6

AUSGEZEICHNET MIT / AWARDED WITH
DDC GOLD - DEUTSCHER DESIGNER CLUB E.V. FÜR GUTE GESTALTUNG // IF COMMUNICATION DESIGN AWARD 2012 BEST OF CORPORATE PUBLISHING // ADC BRONZE // RED DOT BEST OF THE BEST & D&AD // NOMINIERT FÜR DEN DEUTSCHEN DESIGNPREIS 2015 // WINNER AUTOMOTIVE BRAND CONTEST 2014 // GOOD DESIGN AWARD 2014

AUSGEZEICHNETE GESTALTUNG DDC DEUTSCHER DESIGNER CLUB
iF communication design award 2012
Best of Corporate Publishing 2012
reddot design award best of the best 2012
WINNER AUTOMOTIVE BRAND CONTEST 2014
German Design Award NOMINEE 2015

CURVES AUSGABEN / OTHER ISSUES OF CURVES

PYRENÄEN
PYRENEES
Im Handel erhältlich/Available in stores

ÖSTERREICH
AUSTRIA
Im Handel erhältlich/Available in stores

SCHWEIZ
SWITZERLAND
Im Handel erhältlich/Available in stores

SCHOTTLAND
SCOTLAND
Im Handel erhältlich/Available in stores

FRANKREICH
FRANCE
Im Handel erhältlich/Available in stores

USA • KALIFORNIEN
USA • CALIFORNIA
Im Handel erhältlich/Available in stores

SIZILIEN
Im Handel erhältlich/Available in stores

NORTHERN ITALY
Im Handel erhältlich/Available in stores

GERMANY/DENMARK
Im Handel erhältlich/Available in stores

SPAIN • MALLORCA
Im Handel erhältlich/Available in stores

USA • COLORADO/UTAH
Im Handel erhältlich/Available in stores

THAILAND
THAILAND
Im Handel erhältlich/Available in stores

SÜDDEUTSCHALND
SOUTHERN GERMANY
Im Handel erhältlich/Available in stores

S PO 1882